THE SALAFĪ

Its Definition, Dist
Its Call Towa

The Noble Shaykh,
Dr. Muḥammad Ibn ʿUmar Bāzmūl
[Member of the Faculty of Teachers at *Umm al-Qurā* University, the Department of the Book (*al-Qurʾān*) and the *Sunnah* within the College of *Daʿwah* and *Uṣūl al-Dīn*]

First Edition: 1431H/August 2010CE

Cover Design:
Hikma Design Studio
Hikma.Design@Gmail.com

ISBN: 978-0-9828084-1-2

Published by:
Sunnah Publishing
Grand Rapids MI, USA
Admin@SunnahPublishing.net

Our Website:
Http://www.SunnahPublishing.net

فهرس

Table of Contents

Shaykh Muḥammad Bāzmūl's Permission For the Translation and Publication of this Book

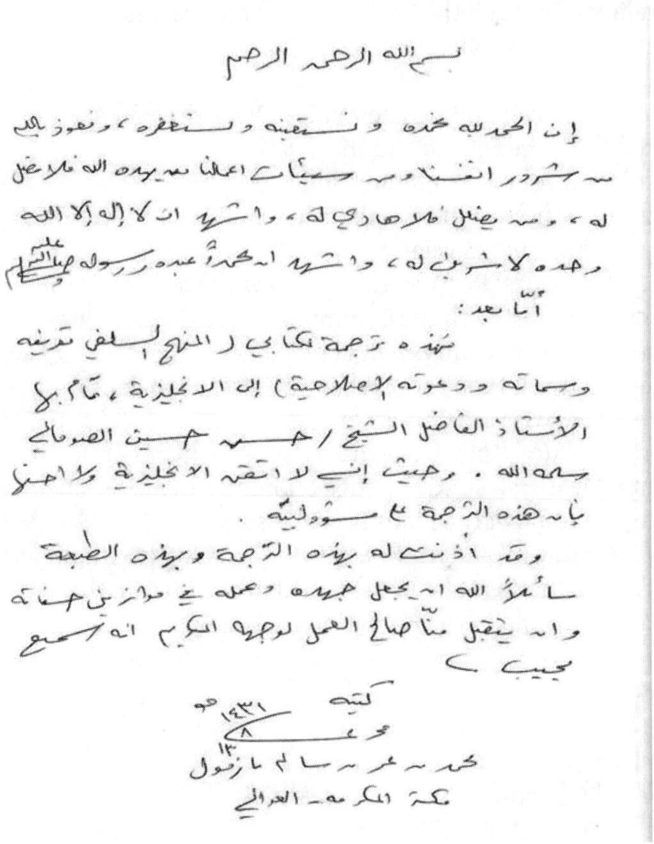
بسم الله الرحمن الرحيم

إن الحمد لله نحمده ونستعينه ونستغفره، ونعوذ بالله
من شرور أنفسنا ومن سيئات أعمالنا من يهده الله فلا مضل
له، ومن يضلل فلا هادي له، وأشهد أن لا إله إلا الله
وحده لا شريك له، وأشهد أن محمداً عبده ورسوله صلى الله عليه وسلم

أما بعد:

فهذه ترجمة لكتابي (المنهج السلفي تعريفه
وسماته ودعوته الإصلاحية) إلى الإنجليزية، قام بها
الأستاذ الفاضل الشيخ / حسن حسين الصومالي
سلمه الله. وحيث إنني لا أتقن الإنجليزية فلا أضمن
بأن هذه الترجمة على مسؤوليته.

وقد أذنت له بهذه الترجمة وبهذه الطبعة
سائلاً الله أن يجعل جهده وعمله في موازين حسناته
وأن يتقبل منا صالح العمل لوجهه الكريم إنه سميع
مجيب.

كتبه

١٤٣١هـ / ٨ / ١٤

محمد بن عمر بن سالم بازمول

مكة المكرمة - العوالي

Scan of the Original Arabic

With the Name of Allāh, the Most Merciful, the Bestower of Mercy

Indeed, the praise is for Allāh. We praise Him, we seek His aid and His forgiveness. We seek refuge with Allāh from the evils of our own souls and from our evil deeds. Whomsoever Allāh guides, then none can misguide him and whosoever Allāh misguides, then none can guide him. And I testify that none has the right to be worshipped besides Allāh alone, without any partner, and I further testify that Muḥammad is His servant and Messenger (ﷺ).

To proceed:

So this is a translation of my book, *The Salafī Methodology: Its Definition, Distinct Characteristics and its Call Towards Rectification*, into the English language. It was carried out by [...][1] Hasan Husayn as-Somali – may Allāh keep him safe. And since I am not proficient in the English language and I am not grounded in it, then the translation is his responsibility. Indeed, I have given him permission for this translation and the printing of this book.[2] I ask Allāh to place his effort and his action in his scale of good deeds and to accept from us righteous deeds done for His noble Face. Indeed, He is the All-Hearing, the One who answers the supplication.

Written by:
Muḥammad Ibn 'Umar Sālim Bāzmūl
13 of Rajab, 1431H
Makkah al-Mukarramah, al-'Awālī

◆◆❖◆◆

[1] **Publisher's Note:** The honorific titles mentioned here were left out at the request of our brother, Hasan as-Somali.
[2] **Publisher's Note:** The translation of this book was a co-operative effort between brothers: Hasan as-Somali and Qaasim Mutiva.

بسم الله الرحمن الرحيم

Indeed, all praise is due to Allāh. We praise Him, seek His aid, assistance and His forgiveness. We seek refuge in Allāh from the evil within ourselves and the evil of our actions. Whoever Allāh guides cannot be led astray and whoever Allāh misguides then no one can guide him. I bear witness that there is nothing worthy of worship except for Allāh without any partner. And I bear witness that Muḥammad (ﷺ) is His servant and Messenger.

﴿ يَٰٓأَيُّهَا ٱلَّذِينَ ءَامَنُوا۟ ٱتَّقُوا۟ ٱللَّهَ حَقَّ تُقَاتِهِۦ وَلَا تَمُوتُنَّ إِلَّا وَأَنتُم
مُّسْلِمُونَ ١٠٢ ﴾

"O you who believe, fear Allāh as He should be feared and do not die except as Muslims."
[Sūrah Āli-ʿImrān 3:102]

﴿ يَٰٓأَيُّهَا ٱلنَّاسُ ٱتَّقُوا۟ رَبَّكُمُ ٱلَّذِى خَلَقَكُم مِّن نَّفْسٍ وَٰحِدَةٍ وَخَلَقَ
مِنْهَا زَوْجَهَا وَبَثَّ مِنْهُمَا رِجَالًا كَثِيرًا وَنِسَآءً ۚ وَٱتَّقُوا۟ ٱللَّهَ ٱلَّذِى
تَسَآءَلُونَ بِهِۦ وَٱلْأَرْحَامَ ۚ إِنَّ ٱللَّهَ كَانَ عَلَيْكُمْ رَقِيبًا ١ ﴾

"O people, fear your Lord who created you from a single soul and created from this soul its mate and sent forth from the two of them many men and women. And fear your Lord through whom you demand your mutual rights, and [fear Allāh] concerning the ties of kinship. Indeed, Allāh is always observing you."

[Sūrah al-Nisā' 4:1]

﴿ يَٰٓأَيُّهَا ٱلَّذِينَ ءَامَنُواْ ٱتَّقُواْ ٱللَّهَ وَقُولُواْ قَوْلًا سَدِيدًا ﴿٧٠﴾ يُصْلِحْ لَكُمْ أَعْمَٰلَكُمْ وَيَغْفِرْ لَكُمْ ذُنُوبَكُمْ ۗ وَمَن يُطِعِ ٱللَّهَ وَرَسُولَهُۥ فَقَدْ فَازَ فَوْزًا عَظِيمًا ﴿٧١﴾ ﴾

"O you who believe, fear Allāh and speak directly and forthright. He will rectify your affairs and forgive you of your sins. And whoever obeys Allāh and His Messenger has [truly] achieved a great achievement."

[Sūrah al-Aḥzāb 33:70-71]

As to what follows:

The most truthful speech is the speech of Allāh, and the best guidance is the guidance of Muḥammad. The most evil of affairs are the newly invented matters and all newly invented matters are considered religious innovation (*bid'ah*) and every religious innovation (*bid'ah*) is misguidance and all misguidance is in the Hellfire.

To proceed: This is a book that was written concerning *the Salafī* methodology, its definition, distinct characteristics and its call towards rectification. I presented it to those of my brothers who were participating in the scholarly educational seminar in al-Zulfī in the year 1429 H/2008 CE during the Islāmic month of *Rabī' al-Thānī* from the 26th to the 28th [May 2nd-4th].

I have compiled it to include three primary objectives and a conclusion.

The First Objective: The definition of the *Salafī* methodology, its principles, the ruling concerning adhering to it and the mention of its virtue.

The Second Objective: The distinguishing characteristics of the *Salafī* methodology.

The Third Objective: The call towards rectification that exists within the *Salafī* methodology.

The Conclusion: Words of some of the Imāms pertaining to adhering to the *Sunnah* and learning the Religion.

I ask that Allāh grants everyone success, steadfastness and guidance.

The First Objective
The Definition of the *Salafī* Methodology, its Principles, the Ruling Concerning Adhering To it and the Mention of its Virtue

The word 'methodology (*manhaj*)' refers to a way and a clear path. In this context, it is considered a pathway and a clearly defined course that leads towards the knowledge of a particular affair. The term *Salafī* is an ascription to the *Salaf*. In the Arabic language everyone who preceded you from your forefathers and relatives are considered your *Salaf* [predecessors]. The plural of *Salaf* is *sullāf* or *aslāf*. The phrase *al-Qawm al-Sullāf* [in Arabic] means: The people who have preceded you.

An example of this is ʿAbd al-Raḥmān Ibn ʿAbdullāh al-Salafī (d.576H) the famous Scholar of *ḥadīth*, and there are others from amongst the Scholars of the past who have formally used this ascription to the *Salaf* [the pious predecessors].

So the intended meaning here is what the Messenger of Allāh (ﷺ) was upon, his Companions and those who followed them upon righteousness.

Therefore, the *Salafī* methodology is the path through which devout observance of the way of the Messenger (ﷺ) and his companions can be achieved. Or [it can also be said that] the *Salafī* Methodology is to traverse upon the path of the Companions and imitate them in the way that they used to follow the Messenger (ﷺ) and apply the narrations.

Linguistically, *Salafī* is an ascription to the *Salaf*. This term can often be found in the speech of the people of knowledge in many places. The term *Salafiyyah* [or salafism] is what the people of *ḥadīth* are upon, those who are the people of the *Sunnah* and the *Jamāʿah*. These are some of the names that are used to describe the people of the *Sunnah* and the *Jamāʿah*:

- *Ahl al-Ḥadīth* (The people of *ḥadīth*)
- *Ahl al-Sunnah wa al-Jamāʿah*
- *Al-Salafiyūn*
- *Atbāʿ al-Salaf* (The followers of the *Salaf*)

Allāh (سبحانه وتعالى) said:

﴿ وَمَن يُشَاقِقِ ٱلرَّسُولَ مِنۢ بَعْدِ مَا تَبَيَّنَ لَهُ ٱلْهُدَىٰ وَيَتَّبِعْ غَيْرَ سَبِيلِ
ٱلْمُؤْمِنِينَ نُوَلِّهِۦ مَا تَوَلَّىٰ وَنُصْلِهِۦ جَهَنَّمَ ۖ وَسَآءَتْ مَصِيرًا ﴿١١٥﴾ ﴾

> **"And whoever opposes the Messenger after guidance has been made clear to him, and follows other than the way of the Believers; We will direct him towards the path which he has chosen, and burn him in Hell - and what an evil destination.."** [Sūrah al-Nisāʾ 4:115]

The way of the believers is firstly and foremostly describing what the Companions were upon. So abandonment of their way is deemed as following other than the path of the Believers.

The Messenger of Allāh (ﷺ) said, "Cling to my *Sunnah* and the way of the rightly guided *Khulafāʾ* [Caliphs] who will come after me[1]"

Abū Ḥātim Ibn Ḥibbān (d.354H) - رحمه الله - stated, "In his statement (ﷺ), "Cling to my *Sunnah*," which he (ﷺ) mentioned when speaking about the differing that will occur within his *Ummah* is a clear illustration that whoever continuously sticks to the *Sunnah*, speaks in accordance with it and does not turn away from it [to delve into] opinions will be from the

---

[1] This *ḥadīth* is *Ḥasan* (sound). It is narrated upon the authority of al-ʿIrbāḍ Ibn Sāriyah (رضي الله عنه). It was collected by Aḥmad in the *Musnad* (4/126-127), al-Dārimī (no. 2676) in the introduction, al-Tirmidhī (no. 2676), Abū Dāwūd (no. 4607), and Ibn Mājah (no. 42 and 45). Al-Albānī has authenticated this narration in *Irwāʾ al-Ghalīl* (8/107, no. 2455).

Saved Sect on the Day of Resurrection - may Allāh favour us to be amongst them."

Then he [Abū Ḥātim Ibn Ḥibbān] entitled a chapter, 'A mention of the narrations that explain what is obligatory upon the individual as it relates to adherence to the *Sunan* of Muḥammad (ﷺ), and safeguarding oneself from anyone who rejects [the *Sunan*] from the people of innovation (*bid'ah*), even if they attempt to beautify this and make it seem pleasing to his eye.'[1]

Thawbān stated that the Messenger of Allāh (ﷺ) said, "There will always remain a group from my *Ummah* steadfast and manifest upon the truth. They are unharmed by those who desert them and they will remain like this until the order of Allāh is established."[2]

Abū 'Īsā al-Tirmidhī (d.274H) said, "This *ḥadīth* is *Ḥasan Ṣaḥīḥ*. I heard Muḥammad Ibn Ismā'īl say: I heard 'Alī Ibn al-Madīnī (d.234H) say...He mentioned this *ḥadīth*, 'There will always remain a group from my nation steadfast and manifest upon the truth.' 'Alī said: 'They are the people of *Ḥadīth*.'"[3]

Mu'āwiyyah Ibn Abī Sufyān stood up amongst us and said, "Indeed the Messenger of Allāh (ﷺ) stood up before us and said, 'Verily, those who preceded you from the People of the Book divided into seventy-two sects; and this nation will divide into seventy-three sects. Seventy-two of these sects will inhabit the Hellfire and one will be in Paradise. And this is the *Jamā'ah*.[4]'"

---

[1] *Ṣaḥīḥ Ibn Ḥibbān* (1/180).

[2] This *ḥadīth* is *mutawātir*, refer to *Iqtiḍā' al-Ṣirāṭ al-Mustaqīm* (p. 6) and *Naẓm al-Mutanāthir min al-Ḥadīth al-Mutawātir* (p. 93).

[3] *Sunan al-Tirmidhī* (no. 2229).

[4] *Ṣaḥīḥ li ghayrhi* (authentic due to supporting narrations) and some have pointed to the fact that it could be considered *mutawātir*. It was collected by Aḥmad in his *Musnad* (4/102), Abū Dāwūd (no. 4597) and al-Ājurrī in his book *al-Shar'iyyah* (1/132, no. 31) of the checked edition. This narration has been authenticated by the person who checked the book *Jāmi' al-Uṣūl* (10/32) and by al-Albānī in *Silsilah al-Aḥādīth al-Ṣaḥīḥah* (no. 204). Al-Albānī also mentioned a number of *ḥadīth* that strengthen this narration. Refer to *Naẓm al-Mutanāthir min al-Ḥadīth al-Mutawātir* →

Al-Tirmidhī reported upon the authority of ʿAbdullāh Ibn ʿUmar that the Messenger of Allāh (ﷺ) said, "There will come a time for my nation which will resemble what befell the children of Isrāʾīl step by step. Verily, the children of Isrāʾīl divided into seventy-two sects; and this nation will divide into seventy-three sects. All of them will reside in the Hellfire except for one. They asked: 'Who are they O Messenger of Allāh?' He replied: 'Those who are upon what I am upon and my Companions.'"

◆◆❖◆◆

(p. 32-34). Refer to *The Status of the People of Hadeeth - Their Feats and Praiseworthy Effects in the Religion* by Rabīʾ Ibn Hādī, Salafi Publications.

The Fundamental Principles of *Salafiyyah*

The *Salafī* methodology stands upon three fundamental principles:

1. **The First:** Sincerely directing all worship to Allāh (ﷻ) alone.
2. **The Second:** Holding fast to the *Jamāʿah*, and hearing and obeying [the Muslim rulers].
3. **The Third:** Being extremely cautious of innovation (*bidʿah*) and the people of religious innovation.

From the evidences that provide textual support for these fundamental principles is the following:

Al-ʿIrbāḍ Ibn Sāriyah (رضي الله عنه) said, "The Messenger of Allāh (ﷺ) admonished us one day after the early morning prayer. The admonition was heartfelt and eloquent and caused the eyes to shed tears and the hearts to tremble. A man from amongst us said, 'Certainly, it is as if this is a farewell admonition, so with what do you advise us, O Messenger of Allāh (ﷺ)?' He replied, 'I advise you to fear Allāh and to listen and obey those in authority over you even if it were an Abyssinian slave. Indeed, whoever from amongst you lives long will witness much differing. And beware of newly invented matters for surely they are misguidance. Whoever from amongst you lives to witness this, then cling to my *Sunnah* and the way of the rightly guided *Khulafāʾ* [Caliphs] who will come after me and grab hold of it with your molar teeth.[1]'"

Suhayl Ibn Abī Ṣāliḥ said upon the authority of his father who narrated from Abū Hurayrah (رضي الله عنه) that the Messenger of Allāh (ﷺ) said, "Indeed, Allāh loves for you three things and despises for you three things. He loves for you that you worship Him alone and that you do not associate any partners with him; that you hold on to the rope of Allāh altogether; and that you advise those who have been placed in authority over you.

---

[1] This *ḥadīth* is established and the sources have already been mentioned.

Allāh despises for you gossip, the wasting of wealth and incessant questioning."[1]

These three principles have been explicitly mentioned in the narration of Zayd Ibn Thābit (⌖) who said, "I heard the Messenger of Allāh (⌖) say, 'Allāh will brighten the face of the one who hears from us a *ḥadīth* (narration), memorizes it and then conveys it to others. Perhaps, the one who conveys it does not comprehend it, and perhaps the one carrying *fiqh* conveys it to one who has more understanding than himself. There are three characteristics which when present the heart of a Muslim will never harbor any vindictive feelings: Sincerely performing an action for Allāh, advising those who have been placed in authority over you and holding fast to the *Jamāʿah*. Indeed their call protects all those behind them.'"[2]

These three characteristics encompass everything that the people's Religion and their worldly affairs are built upon. Shaykhul-Islām Muḥammad Ibn ʿAbdul-Wahhāb (d.1206H) said, "There is no deficiency in a person's Religion or worldly affairs except due to a discrepancy in these three things or some of them."[3]

There is no doubt that following the legislation of Islām requires abandonment of innovation (*bidʿah*) and its people. Here is an explanation of these principles:

◆◆❖◆◆

---

[1] Related by Mālik in his *Muwaṭṭa* (no. 1863), Aḥmad in his *al-Musnad* and collected by Muslim (no. 1715) without his saying, "And that you advise those who have been placed in authority over you."

[2] This *ḥadīth* has been transmitted with chains which are authentic, chains which are *ḥasan* (sound) and others which are *maʿlūlah* (defective) upon a group of the Companions. This *ḥadīth* is *mutawātir* (frequently narrated). Refer to the treatise *Dirāsah Ḥadīth Naḍḍara Allāh ʾImraʾan* by Shaykh ʿAbdul-Muḥsin al-ʿAbbād.

[3] *Masāʾil al-Jāhiliyyah*, which is part of the collection entitled *Majmūʿ al-Tawḥīd al-Najdiyyah*; al-Maktabah al-Salafiyyah print, Egypt, (p. 236-237).

The First Principle
Establishing the Worship of Allāh (ﷻ) Through Adherence to the Book (the *Qur'ān*) and the *Sunnah* According to the Understanding of the Pious Predecessors (*al-Salaf al-Ṣāliḥ*)

Establishing this involves solely worshipping Allāh without directing worship to other than Him, and to only worship Him in the manner that He has legislated. This is the actualization of the phrase which indicates absolute sincerity, "I bear witness that there is nothing worthy of worship except for Allāh; and I bear witness that Muḥammad (ﷺ) is His servant and Messenger." Thus, the Religion is established upon two foundations:

1. That we do not worship anything except Allāh.
2. That we do not worship Allāh except in the manner that He legislated.

This is the first fundamental principle that the *Salafī* methodology is built upon: The establishment of Allāh's worship by following His legislation. Those who oppose this stray away from the Straight Path.

Abū Hurayrah (رضي الله عنه) narrated that the Messenger of Allāh (ﷺ) said, "Indeed I have left behind me two things and you will never go astray after them: The Book of Allāh (the *Qur'ān*) and my *Sunnah*. The two will never separate until they meet me at the *Ḥawḍ* (Pool)."[1]

Ibn ʿAbbās (رضي الله عنهما) narrated that, "The Messenger of Allāh (ﷺ) delivered a *khuṭbah* (sermon) to the people during his farewell sermon wherein he said, 'O people, I have left you with something that if you adhere to it,

---

[1] Collected by al-Dāraquṭnī in his *Sunan* (4/245), *al-Mustadrak* (1/284, no. 324) and al-Bayhaqī in *al-Sunan al-Kubrā* (10/114). It was also mentioned in *Majmaʿ al-Zawā'id* (9/163). This *ḥadīth* is raised to the level of *Ḥasan li ghayrihi* (sound due to other supporting narrations).

you will never be misguided: The Book of Allāh (the *Qur'ān*) and the *Sunnah* of His Prophet (ﷺ)."'[1]

Kathīr Ibn ʿAbdullāh Ibn ʿAmr Ibn ʿAwf narrated from his father who narrated from his grandfather that the Messenger of Allāh (ﷺ) said, "I have left you with two things you will never stray so long as you cling to them: The Book of Allāh (the *Qur'ān*) and the *Sunnah* of His Prophet (ﷺ).[2]"

Whoever clings to the Book of Allāh (the *Qur'ān*) and the *Sunnah* will be guided. The Companions were the most knowledgeable people concerning them both. So whoever follows the Book of Allāh (the *Qur'ān*) and the *Sunnah* upon the understanding of the pious predecessors (*al-Salaf al-Ṣāliḥ*) will be safe.

◆◆❖◆◆

---

[1] Related by al-Bayhaqī; see the previous footnote.
[2] Related by Ibn ʿAbd al-Barr in his book *al-Tamhīd*.

The Second Principle
Holding Fast to the *Jamā'ah*, and Hearing And Obeying [the Muslim Rulers]

The [People of *Sunnah*] hold fast to the *Jamā'ah* and fulfil the rights of those who have been placed in authority, and the greatest of these rights and the most serious of them is obeying those in authority so long as they do not command with disobedience.[1]

Allāh (ﷻ) said,

﴿ يَٰٓأَيُّهَا ٱلَّذِينَ ءَامَنُوٓاْ أَطِيعُواْ ٱللَّهَ وَأَطِيعُواْ ٱلرَّسُولَ وَأُوْلِي ٱلۡأَمۡرِ مِنكُمۡۖ فَإِن تَنَٰزَعۡتُمۡ فِي شَيۡءٖ فَرُدُّوهُ إِلَى ٱللَّهِ وَٱلرَّسُولِ إِن كُنتُمۡ تُؤۡمِنُونَ بِٱللَّهِ وَٱلۡيَوۡمِ ٱلۡأٓخِرِۚ ذَٰلِكَ خَيۡرٞ وَأَحۡسَنُ تَأۡوِيلًا ﴿٥٩﴾ ﴾

"O you who believe! Obey Allāh and obey the Messenger, and those in authority from among you. And if you differ in anything amongst yourselves, then refer it back to Allāh and His Messenger, if you believe in Allāh and in the Last Day. That is the best and most suitable determination." [Sūrah al-Nisā' 4:59]

---

[1] The meaning of the statement "There is no obedience to the ruler if he commands with something which is considered disodience to Allāh," is that there is no obedience in that particular affair which involves disobeying Allāh. So if he [the ruler] commands with something that is impermissible, then it is compulsory that he not be obeyed in that affair because obeying Allāh is the greater of rights. However, it should not be understood from this that if he commands with disobedience that there is no hearing and obeying him whatsoever. Rather, he is to be absolutely obeyed unless he commands with disobedience, and in that specific scenario he is not to be heared or obeyed. Refer to *Mu'āmalah al-Hukkām* (p. 78).

In this *āyah* is proof that it is obligatory to hear and obey [those in authority] when they command with something so long as it does not oppose obedience to Allāh and His Messenger (ﷺ).

ʿAlī (رضي الله عنه) narrated that the Messenger of Allāh (ﷺ) dispatched a military party and appointed a man from the *Anṣār* as its leader. He commanded them to obey the man who was appointed. Later the man who was appointed to lead them became angry and said, "Didn't the Prophet (ﷺ) command you all to obey me?" They responded saying, "Of course." He then said, "Then I have decided that after you have gathered firewood and started a fire, you should enter into it." So they gathered the firewood and started the fire but when they were just about to enter the fire, they began to look at one another. Some of them said, "Certainly, we have followed the Prophet (ﷺ) in an effort to flee the fire so should we really enter it?" While they were in this state, the cinders of the fire died down and the anger of their appointed leader abated. This was mentioned to the Prophet (ﷺ) and he said, "If they had entered into that fire, they would never have left it. Obedience is only to be observed in the matters that are good."

Ibn ʿUmar (رضي الله عنهما) narrated that the Prophet (ﷺ) said, "Hearing and obeying is obligatory so long as [a person] is not commanded with disobedience. If someone is commanded with disobedience, then there is no hearing or obeying."[1]

The Messenger (ﷺ) placed a great deal of emphasis upon the importance of obeying the Muslim leader to the extent that he made holding fast to the *Jamāʿah* of the Muslims and their leader a means of safeguarding oneself from the callers to the gates of the Hellfire.

Busr Ibn ʿUbayd Allāh al-Ḥaḍramī said: Abū Idrīs al-Khawlānī said that he heard Ḥudhayfah Ibn al-Yamān (رضي الله عنه) saying, "The people used to ask the Messenger of Allāh (ﷺ) about the good but I used to ask him about the evil out of fear that it might reach me. So I asked him, 'O Messenger of Allāh (ﷺ), certainly we lived in a period of ignorance and evil, but

---

[1] Related by al-Bukhārī (no. 2955) and Muslim (no. 1839).

Allāh provided us with this good. Will there come after this good any evil?' He said: 'Yes.' I said: 'And after this evil will there be any good?' He said: 'Yes but it will be tainted.' I said: 'What will taint it?' He said: 'There will be a people who seek guidance in other than my guidance. You will recognize some of what you see from them and rebuke other things.' I said: 'Then after that good will there be evil?' He said: 'Yes, callers to the doors of the Hellfire, whoever answers their call will be thrown into it.' I said: 'O Messenger of Allāh (ﷺ), describe them for us.' He said: 'They are from our own people and they speak with our tongue.'[1] I said: 'So with what do you command me if this were to reach me?' He said: 'Hold fast to the *Jamāʿah* of the Muslims and their Imām.' I said: 'What if there is no *Jamāʿah* or an Imām?' He said: 'Then abandon all of the factions even if this means that you have to bite onto the root of a tree until death overtakes you, and you are in this state.'"[2]

In another transmission of this narration we find the obligation of hearing and obeying the Muslim rulers even if they were to take your wealth and beat your backs.

Abū Sallām said: Ḥudhayfah Ibn al-Yamān (ﷺ) said, "I said, 'O Messenger of Allāh (ﷺ), indeed we were in [a period of] evil and Allāh gave us this good that we are currently in. Will any evil appear after this good?' He said: 'Yes.' So I said, 'Will there be any evil after this good?' He said: 'Yes.' So then I said, 'So then will there be any evil that will follow that good?' He said, 'Yes.' I said, 'How [will this occur]?' He said: 'There will appear after me Imāms who do not follow my guidance, nor will they follow my *Sunnah*. There will arise from amongst them men whose hearts are like the hearts of devils yet they are in the bodies of men.' I said, 'How shall I conduct myself, O Messenger of Allāh (ﷺ), if I were to reach such a time?' He said: 'Hear

---

[1] One should pause at the description of the callers to misguidance. The Messenger (ﷺ) instructed us to hold fast to the jamāʿ*ah* when the callers to misguidance are numerous. This is the way to successfully safeguard oneself from the trial and tribulation of these individuals, and not by declaring the leaders of the Muslims to be disbelievers, revolting against them or by turning the hearts of the people against them.

[2] Related by al-Bukhārī (no. 3606).

and obey the leader even if he were to beat your back and take your wealth. Listen and obey!'"[1]

Further support for the narration of Abū Sallām came in the form of a narration transmitted by Khālid Ibn Khālid al-Yashkurī who said, "I set out at a time when Tustar (Shushtar)[2] had been conquered and continued until I arrived in al-Kūfah. I entered the mosque [of al-Kūfah] and found myself in a gathering of individuals and there was one man that stood out. He had nice teeth and was clearly from the men of the Ḥijāz. So I inquired: 'Who is this man?' The people replied: 'Do you not know him?' So I said: 'No.' Then they said: 'This is Ḥudhayfah Ibn al-Yamān, the Companion of the Messenger of Allāh (ﷺ).' Then I sat down while he spoke to the people, and he said: 'Indeed the people used to ask the Messenger of Allāh (ﷺ) about the good but I used to ask him about the evil.' Then the people began to reproach him for this. He then said to them: 'I shall inform you concerning what you have found strange. Islām came at the time that it did and appeared before us as an affair that was distinctly different from the period of ignorance. I was given understanding of the *Qur'ān*, so when men used to come and ask about the good I used to ask [the Prophet (ﷺ)] about the evil. I said to him: 'O Messenger of Allāh (ﷺ), will there come after this good any evil just as there was evil that existed before it?' He said: 'Yes.' I then said: 'Then what will protect us, O Messenger of Allāh (ﷺ)?' He said: 'You will find protection in the sword.' Then I said: 'Will any of this remain after the use of the sword?' He said: 'Yes. There will be corrupt leadership and there will be an unstable agreement.' I said: 'Then what?' He said: 'Then callers to misguidance will come forth. If at that time Allāh has decreed that there should be a *Khalīfah* (Caliph) who beats your back and takes your property, then obey him. Otherwise, you should die biting on to the root of a tree.' I said: 'Then what?' He said: 'The *Dajjāl* (Anti-Christ) will appear with a river and a fire. Whoever enters his fire will receive his reward and be relieved of his burden; and whoever enters his river will be assured of his burden and

---

[1] Related by Muslim (no. 1847).

[2] **Translator's note:** *Tustar* or *Shustar* as it is pronounced in Persian is the greatest city of Khūzestān which is a province of modern day Iran situated near the Kārūn River in southwest Iran. See *Mu'jam al-Buldān* (2/29-31).

be deprived of his reward.' I said: 'Then what?' To which he replied: 'Then a mare will not deliver a foal that can grow old enough to be mounted except that the Hour will be established.'"[1] The term [الصَّدْعُ مِنَ الرِّجَالِ] mentioned in this narration refers to a specific description or type of man.

The Messenger of Allāh (ﷺ) instructed us to obey the Muslim leader even if we see from him things that we dislike to the extent that we should not raise a single hand in disobedience of him.

'Awf Ibn Mālik (رضي الله عنه) narrated that the Messenger of Allāh (ﷺ) said, "The best of your Imāms [leaders] are those whom you love and those who love you; they are those whom you supplicate for and those who supplicate for you. The worst of your Imāms are those whom you dislike and those who dislike you; they are those whom you curse and those who curse you." It was said, 'O Messenger of Allāh (ﷺ), should we not overthrow them with our swords?' Then he said: "No, so long as they establish the prayer amongst you. If you see something from your leaders that you dislike, then you should dislike his action without raising a hand in disobedience."

In a similar narration, "The best of your Imāms are those whom you love and those who love you; they are those whom you supplicate for and those who supplicate for you. The worst of your Imāms are those whom you dislike and those who dislike you; they are those whom you curse and those who curse you." They said, "We said: 'O Messenger of

---

[1] Related by Aḥmad in the *Musnad* (5/386) and Ibn Ḥibbān (*al-Iḥsān,* 13/298). This *ḥadīth* has been authenticated by Ibn Ḥibbān and also the person that checked *al-Iḥsān*. In the completion of this narration comes the wording of his statement: "Then what will protect us, O Messenger of Allāh (ﷺ)? He said: You will find protection in the sword." Qatādah (d.104H) considered this a reference to the apostasy that occurred during the time of Abū Bakr. And concerning his statement, "There will be corrupt leadership and there will be an unstable agreement." This is a reference to a truce. His statement, "unstable or tainted," refers to the existence of resentment and malice. The benefit of this narration is that it provides support for the narration of Abū Sallām who narrated upon Ḥudhayfah. So the [problem of] the breakage in the chain is resolved - and Allāh knows best.

Allāh (ﷺ), should we not overthrow them with our swords if that happens?'" He said, "No, so long as they establish the Prayer amongst you. No, so long as they establish the Prayer amongst you. Whoever has someone placed in authority over him and then witnesses them committing an act of disobedience to Allāh, then they should detest the disobedience of Allāh that he committed but he must not raise a single hand in disobedience."[1]

The Messenger of Allāh (ﷺ) placed great emphasis upon the importance of hearing and obeying the Muslim rulers to the extent that he made this issue a means for entering Paradise.

Abū Hurayrah (رضي الله عنه) narrated that the Messenger of Allāh (ﷺ) said, "All of my nation will enter Paradise except for those who refuse." They said, 'And who would refuse?' He said, "Whoever obeys me enters Paradise and whoever disobeys me has certainly refused."[2]

Abū Hurayrah (رضي الله عنه) narrated that the Messenger of Allāh (ﷺ) said, "Whoever obeys me has obeyed Allāh and whoever disobeys me has disobeyed Allāh. Whoever obeys my *amīr* (appointed leader) has obeyed me and whoever disobeys my *amīr* has disobeyed me."[3]

So examine - may Allāh have mercy upon you - how the Messenger of Allāh (ﷺ) established a connection between obeying him and obeying the Muslim leader, and disobeying him and disobeying the Muslim leader. Similarly, examine the way that he established a connection between his obedience and entering Paradise, and likewise his disobedience and refusing to enter Paradise.

The end result is: Whoever obeys the Muslim leader has obeyed the Messenger (ﷺ), and whoever obeys the Messenger (ﷺ) enters Paradise. Whoever disobeys the Muslim leader has clearly disobeyed the

---

[1] Related by Muslim (no. 1855).
[2] Related by al-Bukhārī (no. 7280) and Muslim (no. 1835).
[3] Related by al-Bukhārī (no. 7137) and Muslim (no. 1835).

Messenger (ﷺ), and whoever disobeys the Messenger (ﷺ) has clearly refused to enter Paradise.

The Messenger of Allāh (ﷺ) considered the abandonment of the solemn pledge of support (*bayʿah*) and disobeying the Muslim leader abandonment of the *Jamāʿah* [community] of the Muslims; and this is a door that leads to leaving the Religion.

ʿAbdullāh narrated that the Messenger of Allāh (ﷺ) said, "The blood of a Muslim who bears witness that there is nothing worthy of worship except for Allāh and that I am the Messenger of Allāh (ﷺ) is forbidden except in three circumstances: The married adulterer, a life for a life, and the one who has abandoned his Religion and has forsaken the *Jamāʿah*."[1]

Look at the way that the Messenger (ﷺ) linked abandonment of the religion to forsaking the *Jamāʿah*.

Ibn ʿAbbās (رضي الله عنه) narrated that the Prophet (ﷺ) said, "Whoever witnesses something from his leader that he dislikes let him remain patient since the one who forsakes the *Jamāʿah* the distance of a hand span and dies in that state does not die except in a state of *Jāhiliyyah* (pre-Islāmic ignorance)."[2]

Nāfiʿ (d.117H) said, "ʿAbdullāh Ibn ʿUmar came to ʿAbdullāh Ibn Muṭīʿ during the events of al-Ḥarrah at the time of Yazīd Ibn Muʿāwiyah and he said: 'Lay down a cushion for Abū ʿAbd al-Raḥmān.' So he said: 'I have not come to you to sit. I came to you to inform you of a narration that I heard from the Messenger of Allāh (ﷺ). I heard the Messenger of Allāh (ﷺ) say: 'Whoever removes a single hand from obedience [to the Muslim leader] will meet Allāh on the day of Resurrection with no argument in his defense. Whoever dies without having offered the

---

[1] Related by al-Bukhārī (no. 6878) and Muslim (no. 1676) and the wording is that of Muslim.

[2] Related by al-Bukhārī (no. 7054) and by Muslim (no. 1848).

solemn pledge of support (*bay'ah*) has died the death of *Jāhiliyyah* (pre-Islāmic ignorance).'"[1]

Look closely - may Allāh grant you success in attaining the truth - at how the Messenger (ﷺ) placed such great emphasis on the issue of obeying the Muslim leader in permissible affairs and how he warned against disobeying him.

Another example of this is the *ḥadīth* narrated by 'Irbāḍ Ibn Sāriyah (رضي الله عنه) who said, "The Messenger of Allāh (ﷺ) addressed us after the early morning Prayer with an eloquent admonition that caused the eyes to shed tears and the hearts to tremble. Then a man said: 'It is as if this is a farewell admonition so what do you advise us with?' He said: 'I advise you all to fear Allāh and listen and obey [the Muslim leader] even if he were an Abyssinian slave. For indeed, whoever lives long from amongst you will witness much differing. And beware of newly invented matters [in the Religion] since they are clearly misguidance. Whoever from amongst you reaches that time, must adhere to my *Sunnah* and the *Sunnah* of the rightly guided *Khulafā'* (Caliphs) who will come after me. Bite onto this with your molar teeth.'"[2]

This was his farewell advice in which he sufficed by focusing upon the following matters:

- The command to fear Allāh which will rectify that which is between the servant and his Lord.
- The command to hear and obey the leader of the Muslims even if he were an Abyssinian slave. This affair will rectify the matters of a Muslim's worldly life as well as his community.
- He further advised the people concerning what they should do when they are faced with a situation which is contrary to what was established during his lifetime (ﷺ) from the fear of Allāh and hearing and obeying the leader of the Muslims. [He advised

---

[1] Related by Muslim (no. 1851).
[2] This *ḥadīth* is established and the sources have already been mentioned.

them if they were to witness this] to return to the *Sunnah* of the Messenger (ﷺ) and the *Sunnah* of the rightly guided *Khulafāʾ* (Caliphs). When this approach is adopted, then rectification can continue and the corruption that manifests can be eliminated along with any change in the community as it relates to the two previously mentioned issues, fearing Allāh and hearing and obeying the Muslim leader.

In this narration is a proof that this is an important [matter] and that it is an obligation. Look at how these issues were expressed with nominal sentences as opposed to verbal sentences. He did not say for example, "I advise you to fear Allāh and to hear and obey [in this present time] even if an Abyssinian slave was given authority over you." Rather, the narration was transmitted in the context of a nominal sentence so the Prophet (ﷺ) said, "I advise you all to fear Allāh and to hear and obey [at all times]..." It was expressed - and Allāh knows best - with the usage of nominal sentences because this indicates that [this advice and direction] is continuous, established and unchangeable as opposed to verbal sentences which can indicate the occurrence of an action and its repetition without indicating continuity. Therefore, this highlights that the Muslim is required to consistently fit this description [i.e. he should always fear Allāh, and hear and obey those in authority] until it becomes something that is continuous, firmly established and decisive. All of this reinforces the importance of fearing Allāh, holding fast to the *Jamāʿah*, and hearing and obeying the Muslim leaders without rebelling against them.

If the situation is one where holding fast to the *Jamāʿah* is promoted and dissention and differing is considered blameworthy, then this means that there must be a united *Jamāʿah*. It has been transmitted from Tamīm al-Dārī (رضي الله عنه) that he said, "The people competed with one another during the time of ʿUmar in the construction of tall buildings. So ʿUmar said: 'O Arabs; this land, this land! Verily, there is no Islām without a *Jamāʿah*; there is no *Jamāʿah* without leadership; and there is no leadership without obedience. Whoever is promoted by his own people based upon knowledge and understanding, then this is life for both him and them. But whoever is promoted by his people based upon other than knowledge and understanding, then this is destruction for both him and them.'"[1]

[It is well known in the Religion of Islām by necessity that there can be no Religion except with a *Jamāʿah*; there can be no *Jamāʿah* except with leadership; and there can be no leadership without listening and obeying. [It is also known that] rebellion against the Muslim leader and any attempts to overthrow him are from the greatest of ways to cause corruption in the land and amongst the people; and it ultimately leads people away from the path of guidance and uprightness.[2]

Al-Ḥasan al-Baṣrī (d.110H) said, "By Allāh, the Religion cannot prevail except by way of the Muslim leaders, even if they are tyrannical and oppressive. By Allāh, Allāh will rectify by way of them far more than they will corrupt."[3]

Ibn Rajab (d.795H) said, "Hearing and obeying the Muslim leaders results in success in the life of this world and through this the people are able to carry out their daily routines as normal and in an orderly fashion. This is something that assists the servants to outwardly practice their religion and obey their Lord."[4]

Abandoning the obedience of the Muslim leader and any attempts to undermine his authority through revolt or the like of this is 'sinful and in direct opposition to Allāh and His Messenger (ﷺ). This is also considered to be in direct opposition to the methodology of the people of the *Sunnah* and the *Jamāʿah*, the Pious Predecessors from amongst them.'[5]][6]

---

[1] Related by al-Dārimī in *al-Muqadimah* (no 257). This narration is *Ḥasan li ghayrihi* (sound due to the presence of supporting narrations) - if Allāh wills - especially since there are many authentic *ḥadīth* that convey a similar meaning.
[2] Refer to *Naṣīḥah Muhimmah* (p. 23).
[3] Refer to *Jāmiʿ al-ʿUlūm wa al-Ḥikam* (2/117).
[4] Refer to *Jāmiʿ al-ʿUlūm wa al-Ḥikam* (2/117).
[5] Refer to *Naṣīḥah Muhimmah* page 29.
[6] What is found between the brackets is from the treatise *as-Sunnah fīmā Yataʿlaqu bī Walī al-Ummah* (p. 24-25) of Aḥmad Bāzmūl.

It is obligatory to be patient with their oppression:

Ibn Taymiyyah (d.728H) said, "Being patient with the oppression of the Imāms [Muslim leaders] is a fundamental from the fundamentals of the people of the *Sunnah* and the *Jamā'ah*."[1]

This is true because commanding the masses to observe patience with the oppression and transgression of the tyrannical Imāms (leaders) brings about benefits and averts harms, which is in the best interests of the land and its people.

[Advising the Muslim leader is from the most important matters of the Religion as mentioned in the narration of Tamīm Ibn Aws al-Dārī (ﷺ) who said that the Prophet (ﷺ) said, "The Religion is sincere advice. We inquired: To whom? The Messenger of Allāh (ﷺ) said: To Allāh, His Book, His Messenger, the leaders of the Muslims and the common people."[2]

There comes in the *ḥadīth*, "There are three characteristics which when present the heart of a Muslim will never harbor any vindictive feelings: Sincerely performing an action for Allāh, advising those who have been placed in authority over you and holding fast to the *Jamā'ah*. For indeed their call protects all those behind them."[3]

The meaning of this narration is that whoever does these three things possesses a heart that is free of enmity, treachery and resentment.

---

[1] Refer to *al-Majmū'* (28/179), cited by way of the treatise *as-Sunnah fīmā Yata'laqu bī Walī al-Ummah* (p. 49) of Aḥmad Bāzmūl.

[2] Related by Muslim (no. 55).

[3] This *ḥadīth* has been transmitted with chains which are authentic, chains which are *ḥasan* (sound) and others which are *ma'lūlah* (defective) upon a group of the Companions. This *ḥadīth* is *mutawātir*. Refer to the treatise *Dirāsah Ḥadīth Naḍḍara Allāh 'Imra'an* by Shaykh 'Abdul-Muḥsin al-'Abbād.

Abū Nuʿaym al-Aṣbahānī (d.430H) said, "Whoever advises the Muslim leaders and rulers, then he is upon guidance, and whoever deceives them has transgressed and gone astray."[1]][2]

The foundation of the *Jamāʿah* [community] and what firmly unites the hearts together in the face of the terror of civil strife and dissention is *Tawḥīd*.

Based upon this principle, they [the people of *Sunnah*] do not permit the establishment of *Jihād* except with the Imām [leader] or with his expressed permission. This principle is found in the narration of Abū Hurayrah (⬢) who said that the Messenger of Allāh (⬢) said, "Whoever has obeyed me has certainly obeyed Allāh, and whoever disobeys me has certainly disobeyed Allāh. Whoever obeys the leader has certainly obeyed me, and whoever disobeys the leader has certainly disobeyed me. Indeed, the Imām is a shield behind whom the people fight and through whom they protect themselves. If he commands the people to fear Allāh and acts justly, then for this he will be rewarded; and if he does other than this then he will be held accountable."[3]

They fulfil his covenants and they do not transgress against the non-Muslims who were granted safety and security while living under the protection of the Muslim leader. In this they implement what is found in the narration of ʿAbdullāh Ibn ʿAmr (⬢) who narrated that the Prophet (⬢) said, "Whoever kills a non-Muslim who has an agreement with the Muslim state (*muʿāhad*), will not smell the scent of Paradise even though its scent can be detected from a distance of forty years."[4]

Upon the authority of Ṣafwān Ibn Sulaym who narrated from a large number of the children of the Companions of the Messenger of Allāh (⬢) who narrated from their respective fathers that the Messenger of Allāh (⬢) said, "Let it be known that whoever wrongs a non-Muslim who has

---

[1] *Faḍīlatul-ʿĀdilīn* (p. 140).
[2] What is found between the brackets is from the treatise, *al-Sunnah fīmā Yataʿlaqu bī Walī al-Ummah* (p. 63) by Aḥmad Bāzmūl.
[3] Related by al-Bukhārī (no. 2958) and Muslim (no. 1835).
[4] Related by al-Bukhārī (no. 3166).

an agreement with the Muslim state (*mu'āhad*), denies some of his rights, imposes a burden upon him that is more than he can bear or takes something from him without his permission, then I will contend with him on the Day of Resurrection."[1]

They do not revolt against the Imāms (leaders) on the basis of them falling into disobedience nor do they dispute their decisions. They do not declare the Imāms to be disbelievers unless they witness clear disbelief for which they have a clear proof from Allāh.

[Even if they witnessed open disbelief for which they had clear evidence they would still not rebel against the Imāms] except that they were absolutely certain that their rebellion would not bring a greater harm, and that their actions would not bring evil into the land and endanger the people, and that they truly possessed the ability to [successfully change the regime]. If the [above prerequisites were not met] then they would demonstrate restraint and withhold themselves from such actions. They do not treat the Muslim nation as an experiment for trial and error nor as an object about which they can afford to differ.

They are individuals who act upon the narrations of the Prophet (ﷺ).

In fact, the Messenger of Allāh (ﷺ) accepted the pledges of allegiance (*bay'ah*) on the premise of hearing and obeying [the rulers], and avoiding opposition of those in command.

Junādah Ibn Abū Umayyah narrated that, "We entered upon 'Ubādah Ibn al-Ṣāmit while he was sick. We said to him: 'May Allāh rectify your affair, tell us of a narration that Allāh will allow you to benefit from and that you have heard from the Prophet (ﷺ).' He said: 'The Prophet (ﷺ) summoned us and we gave him the pledge of allegiance, and among the conditions on which he took the pledge from us was that we were to listen and obey both at times when we were active and at times when

---

[1] Related by Abū Dāwūd (no. 3052). This *ḥadīth* is considered *Ḥasan* (sound).

we were tired, and at our times of difficulty and at our times of ease; and not to oppose those in authority unless you see them committing open disbelief for which you have a proof from Allāh.'[1]"[2]

Shaykhul-Islām Ibn Taymiyyah (d.728) said, "It is for this reason that from the fundamental principles of the People of the *Sunnah* and the *Jamāʿah* is holding fast to the *Jamāʿah*, the abandonment of fighting the Imāms [leaders] and the abandonment of fighting during times of social unrest and turmoil. As for the people of desires like the *Muʿtazilah*, then they view fighting against the Imāms as one of the fundamental principles of their Religion."[3]

They also never engage in any activities that could lead to disunity [within the ranks of the Muslims] and fill the people's hearts with enmity towards the Muslim rulers. They never openly criticize them from the podium or the pulpit, in lectures, in sittings or gatherings of the people.[4] This is exactly what the previously mentioned texts have

---

[1] This *ḥadīth* lays the prerequisites that have to be met before a Muslim leader can be declared a disbeliever. **[i]:** In his saying "Unless if you see," he is referring to a matter that is perceivable and observed which is visible to the eyes [i.e. apparent]. [ii] Then the Messenger of Allāh (ﷺ) mentioned the act of seeing with the *wāw* that signifies a plural (*jamāʿah*) which would require that this is something not only noticed by a single individual but there must be a group from amongst the Muslims that witness this clear disbelief. **[iii]:** And "disbelief," means that he does not disbelieve if he commits a sin even if it is a major sin. **[iv]:** And "clear," means that it must be apparent. **[v]:** "For which you have a proof concerning from Allah," means that it cannot just be any proof. Rather, the proof must come from Allāh, which means that the evidence should be a clear cut textual proof that must be related, authentic and explicit.

[2] Related by al-Bukhārī (no. 7056) and by Muslim (no. 1709).

[3] Refer to *al-Istiqāmah* (2/215).

[4] The esteemed Scholar, ʿAbd al-ʿAzīz Ibn Bāz (d.1420H) was asked in *al-Maʿlūm min Wājib al-ʿAlāmah bayna al-Ḥākim wa al-Maḥkūm* (question no. 10), "Is it from the methodology of the *Salaf* to criticize the Muslim leaders from the pulpit? What was the methodology of the *Salaf* in respect to advising the Muslim leaders?

The Shaykh responded by saying, "It is not from the methodology of the *Salaf* to publicly announce the mistakes and shortcomings of the Muslim leaders and to mention these things from the pulpits because these things lead to confusion, disorder and the absence of hearing and obeying the Muslim ruler in what is →

good. It also results in debates and disputes which cause harm and brings no benefit. However, the *Salaf* used to offer sincere advice (*naṣīḥah*) in a way where it was between them and the *Muslim* leader and by writing to him or by reaching him through the scholars who keep in touch with him (to advise him) until the ruler is directed towards the good. Repelling the evil occurs without mentioning the doer of the evil. So fornication, drinking of intoxicants and the taking of usury are forbidden and curbed without mentioning the one who does such things. Warding off the evil and warning the people against it is sufficient without it being mentioned that such and such a person does it, whether he is a ruler or other than the ruler.

When the turmoil erupted during the time of ʿUthmān (ﷺ), some of the people said to Usāmah Ibn Zayd (ﷺ): 'Will you not speak to ʿUthmān?' He then replied: 'Why is it that you think that I have not spoken to him unless you are able to hear what I say? Indeed, I will certainly talk to him regarding that which concerns me and him without initiating a matter which I do not love to be the first to initiate.'

When they (i.e. the instigators) opened up the evil in the time of ʿUthmān and rejected ʿUthmān openly, the *fitnah*, the killing and the mischief, which has not ceased to affect the people to this day, was brought about. This caused the *fitnah* to occur between ʿAlī and Muʿāwiyah. These were the reasons why ʿUthmān was killed.

Furthermore a large number of Companions and others beside them were killed due to openly criticising the ruler and the open proclamation of his faults, until the people began to hate the one charged with authority over them and killed him. We ask Allaah for success."

During a discourse with the esteemed Scholar Dr. Ṣāliḥ Ibn Fawzān al-Fawzān - may Allāh preserve him - he was asked in *Ḥiwār maʿ ʿĀlim* (p. 16-18, question no. 5), "Some of the youth of today understand the statement of Allāh,

﴿ وَلَا يَخَافُونَ لَوْمَةَ لَآئِمٍ ﴾

"And they do not fear the blame of the blamers."

[Sūrah al-Māʾidah 5:54]

They understand it as referring to those individuals who mention the mistakes of the leaders and rulers from the pulpit, in front of the masses and in recorded lectures. They restrict enjoining the good and forbidding the evil to this as well. We hope that you might direct these young people - may Allāh guide them - towards the correct path and clarify the proper meaning of this verse of the *Qurʾān* and the ruling concerning those who publicly speak out against the Muslim ruler?"

Shaykh Ṣāliḥ Ibn Fawzān al-Fawzān replied, "Allāh said,

→

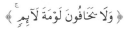

﴿ يَٰٓأَيُّهَا ٱلَّذِينَ ءَامَنُواْ مَن يَرۡتَدَّ مِنكُمۡ عَن دِينِهِۦ فَسَوۡفَ يَأۡتِي ٱللَّهُ بِقَوۡمٖ يُحِبُّهُمۡ
وَيُحِبُّونَهُۥٓ أَذِلَّةٍ عَلَى ٱلۡمُؤۡمِنِينَ أَعِزَّةٍ عَلَى ٱلۡكَٰفِرِينَ يُجَٰهِدُونَ فِي سَبِيلِ ٱللَّهِ
وَلَا يَخَافُونَ لَوۡمَةَ لَآئِمٖۚ ﴾

"O you who believe, whoever from amongst you should commit apostasy and forsake his Religion, then Allāh will bring forth [to replace them] **a people whom He will love and who will love Him. They are humble toward the believers, stern against the disbelievers; they strive for the sake of Allāh and they do not fear the blame of the blamers."** [Sūrah al-Mā'idah 5:54]

This *āyah* refers to those who speak a word of truth, strive for the sake of Allāh, enjoin the good and forbid the evil obediently for Allāh's sake, and they do not abandon sincere advice (*naṣīḥah*), enjoining the good and forbidding the evil, and *Jihād* for the sake of Allāh because of the people or out of fear of the people. However, the issue of sincere advice (*naṣīḥah*) and calling the people to Allāh is as Allāh (ﷻ) said,

﴿ ٱدۡعُ إِلَىٰ سَبِيلِ رَبِّكَ بِٱلۡحِكۡمَةِ وَٱلۡمَوۡعِظَةِ ٱلۡحَسَنَةِۖ وَجَٰدِلۡهُم بِٱلَّتِي هِيَ
أَحۡسَنُۚ ﴾

"Call to the way of your Lord with wisdom and appropriate admonition and argue with them in a manner which is better."
[Sūrah al-Naḥl 16:125]

And Allāh (ﷻ) said to Mūsā and Hārūn when He sent them to Pharaoh,

﴿ فَقُولَا لَهُۥ قَوۡلٗا لَّيِّنٗا لَّعَلَّهُۥ يَتَذَكَّرُ أَوۡ يَخۡشَىٰ ﴿٤٤﴾ ﴾

"And speak to him with gentle speech such that perhaps he may be reminded or fear Allāh." [Sūrah Ṭa Ha 20:44]

And Allāh (ﷻ) said concerning our Prophet Muḥammad (ﷺ),

→

﴿ فَبِمَا رَحْمَةٍ مِّنَ ٱللَّهِ لِنتَ لَهُمْ ۖ وَلَوْ كُنتَ فَظًّا غَلِيظَ ٱلْقَلْبِ لَٱنفَضُّوا۟ مِنْ حَوْلِكَ ۖ ﴾

"So by the mercy of Allāh [O Muḥammad]**, you were lenient with them. And if you had been stern and harsh of heart, they would have disbanded from around you."** [Sūrah Āli-ʿImrān 3:159]

So sincerely advising (*naṣīḥah*) the *Muslim* leaders should be done in an appropriate way that would successfully reach them without being made public or agitating the simpleminded or the masses. Sincere advice (*naṣīḥah*) should be given in secrecy between the advisor and the Muslim leader. It can be given orally, in writing or over the phone. The advisor should clarify these affairs to him with gentleness and the proper manners. As for speaking against the Muslim rulers from the pulpits and in public lectures, then this is not sincere advice (*naṣīḥah*) this is disparagement. This sows the seeds of social unrest and enmity between the Muslim leaders and their nations. This creates a great amount of harm which may result in the leaders scrutinizing the people of knowledge and the callers to Islām due to this behavior. So these actions generate evil and problems which are far greater than the good that it is thought they will bring about. If you noticed that a regular person made a mistake or fell into some type of opposition, and then you went directly to the masses and announced, 'So and so did such and such.' Then this action would be identified as criticism and not advice (*naṣīḥah*). The Prophet (ﷺ) said, 'Whoever conceals the faults of a Muslim, then Allāh will conceal their faults in the worldly life and the hereafter.' If the Prophet (ﷺ) wanted to address the actions of a specific individual, he never identified people by their names. Rather he would say: 'What is the condition of a people that does such and such?' This is because the explicit mention of names creates more corruption than rectification, and perhaps it does not bring about any rectification at all. In fact it tends to create more harm for both the individual as well as the community. The correct manner of offering sincere advice (*naṣīḥah*) is well-known. The people of sincere advice (*naṣīḥah*) who take up this responsibility must possess a certain level of knowledge, understanding, comprehension and the ability to weigh the potential harms against the benefits of different situations. They should possess foresight into what may happen. As forbidding the evil may be a form of evil in itself as Shaykh al-Islām (رحمه الله) said. This occurs when an evil is forbidden in a way that is not legislated. So forbidding the evil itself becomes evil because of the corruption it causes. The same applies to [what some may claim to be] advice (*naṣīḥah*), we may call it criticism, instigation, or provocation of social unrest and turmoil if it is given in an unlegislated fashion."

indicated and it has also been established from the practice of the *Salaf*. For example Usāmah ibn Zayd (ﷺ), when it was said to him, "Will you not enter upon ʿUthmān and speak with him?" He replied by saying, "Do you believe that I have not spoken to him unless I allow you to hear what was said? By Allāh, I have already spoken with him and our speech will remain between me and him without opening an affair that I do not love to be the first one to open."[1]

Likewise, ʿAbdullāh Ibn Abū Awfā, Imām Aḥmad reported a narration concerning him in his *Musnad*.[2] He said: Abū al-Naḍr told us that al-Ḥashraj ibn Nubātah al-ʿAbsī told us that Saʿīd ibn Jumhān told us that he said: "I came to ʿAbdullah ibn Abū Awfā when he was blind and offered him the Islāmic greetings. He said to me, 'Who are you?' I replied saying, 'I am Saʿīd Ibn Jumhān.' He then asked, 'How is your father?' I then said, 'The *Azāriqah* killed him.' He then said, 'May Allāh's curse be upon the *Azāriqah*. May Allāh's curse be upon the *Azāriqah*. The Messenger of Allāh (ﷺ) told us that the Azāriqah are the dogs of the Hellfire.' I responded, 'Is this only referring to the Azāriqah or all of the sects of the Kharijites (*Khawārij*)?' He said, 'Rather, all of the Kharijites (*Khawārij*).' I said, 'Indeed, the Muslim leader oppresses the people and mistreats them.' Then he took my hand and squeezed it very firmly and said, 'Woe unto you O Ibn Jumhān! Stick to the main body of Muslims; stick to the main body of Muslims! If the Muslim leader will listen to you, then you should approach him at his home and inform him of what you know. If he accepts this from you, then [this is one thing] but if not then leave him alone. You are not more knowledgeable than him.'"[3]

◆◆❖◆◆

---

[1] Related by al-Bukhārī (no. 3267) and Muslim (no. 2989), and the wording is that of Muslim.

[2] Refer to *al-Musnad* (4/382).

[3] Related by al-Ḥākim (3/660), aṭ-Ṭayālisī (no. 822), Ibn Abū ʿĀṣim in *al-Sunnah* (no. 905), and Ibn ʿAdī in *al-Kāmil* (2/441) from the narration of al-Ḥashraj.

The Third Principle
Being Extremely Wary of Religious Innovation (*Bidʿah*) and Religious Innovators (*Mubtadiʿūn*)

The adherents to *Salafiyyah* [or Salafism] are cautious and wary of religious innovation (*bidʿah*) and innovators (*mubtadiʿūn*) because the Messenger of Allāh (ﷺ) warned against these things as we find in his statement, "Beware of newly invented matters [in the Religion] for indeed they are clearly misguidance. So whoever witnesses this from amongst you, then cling to my way (*Sunnah*) and the way (*Sunnah*) of my rightly guided successors [Caliphs]. And bite onto it with your molar teeth."[1]

They consider the task of refuting innovation (*bidʿah*) and destroying the misleading façade of the innovators (*mubtadiʿūn*), which is from those righteous actions that benefit others, better than occupying oneself with supererogatory acts of worship that only benefit the individual who performs them.

It was said to Imām Aḥmad (d.241H), "Is the man who fasts, prays and performs *iʿtikāf* [i.e. supererogatory acts] more beloved to you or the one who speaks out concerning the people of innovation (*bidʿah*)?" He said, "If this person fasts, prays, and performs Iʿtikāf, then this only benefits him. However, if he speaks out concerning the people of innovation (*bidʿah*), then this benefits the Muslims, and this is better."[2]

Abū al-Muẓaffar al-Samʿānī (d.489H) said, "We have been commanded to follow and we have been encouraged with this. We have been forbidden from innovating (*bidʿah*) and severely warned against such behavior. The hallmark of the people of the *Sunnah* is their adherence to the pious predecessors (*al-salaf al-sāliḥ*) and their abandonment of

---

[1] This *ḥadīth* is established and the sources have already been mentioned.
[2] Refer to *Majmūʿ Fatāwā* (27/231) of Refer to Ibn Taymiyyah.

everything that constitutes an innovation (*mubtada'*) or a matter from the Religion that appears without precedent (*muḥdath*)."[1]

The protector of the *Sunnah,* [Abū al-Qāsim Ismā'īl Ibn Muḥammad] al-Aṣbahānī (d.430H) said, "It is befitting that a man is cautious of newly invented matters as every newly invented matter [of the Religion] is a religious innovation (*bid'ah*). The *Sunnah* involves believing in the narrations of the Messenger of Allāh (ﷺ) and the abandonment of opposing them with contentious arguments like how and why. Rhetoric and argumentation in affairs of the Religion, and pointless debate is considered a newly invented affair, and it can sow the seeds of doubt in the hearts and prevent them from recognizing that which is true and correct. And true knowledge is not demonstrated by the amount of narrations that are transmitted rather true knowledge involves following and practical application. A person should follow the Companions and their students even if they possess a limited amount of knowledge, and whoever opposes the Companions and their students is misguided even if they possess a vast amount of knowledge."[2]

◆◆❖◆◆

[1] Refer to *al-Intiṣār li Ahl al-Ḥadīth* by Abū al-Muẓaffar al-Sam'ānī by way of the book *Ṣawn al-Manṭaq wa al-Kalām* (p. 158).
[2] Refer to al-*Ḥujjah fī Bayān al-Maḥajjah* (2/437-438).

The *Salafīs* Stay Away from the Gatherings Of the People of Innovation (*Bidʿah*)

It has been narrated that al-Ḥasan said, "Do not sit with a person of innovation (*bidʿah*), for indeed he will make your heart sick."[1]

Sufyān al-Thawrī (d.167H) said, "Whoever sits with a person of innovation (*bidʿah*) cannot escape one of three things: He is a trial and tribulation for others, something may fall into his heart that remains with him and causes him to enter the Hellfire or he will say, 'By Allāh, I do not care about what they say and I have full confidence in myself.' Whoever feels that they are not in need of Allāh to safeguard his religion even for the blinking of an eye, then He will take it from him."[2]

It has been narrated that Ibn ʿAbbās (ﷺ) said, "Do not sit with the people of desires, for indeed sitting with them will cause a disease to spread in the hearts."[3]

For this reason you will find them wary of innovation (*bidʿah*), especially since it is a road to disbelief.

Ibn al-Qayyim (d.751H) said, "Our Shaykh said, 'The reality of disbelief has been married to immoral innovation (*bidʿah*) and they have given birth to a state of loss in the life of this world and the hereafter.' If he overcomes this imposing obstacle and escapes it with the light of the *Sunnah*, and he seeks to stay clear of it by truly adhering to the *Sunnah* and by emulating those who have passed from the illustrious *Salaf* from the Companions and their students who followed them in goodness, and it is rare for these later generations to produce one of these types of people. However, if a person like this is produced, then the people of

---

[1] Refer to *al-Bidaʿ wa al-Nahyu ʿanhā* of Ibn Waḍḍāḥ (p. 104) with the checking of Badr al-Badr and something similar is mentioned on (p. 110).
[2] Refer to *al-Bidaʿ wa al-Nahyu ʿanhā* (p. 104) of Ibn Waḍḍāḥ with the checking of Badr al-Badr.
[3] Refer to *al-Sharīʿah* (p. 60) by al-Ājurrī.

innovation (*bidʿah*) would set their traps and wreak havoc; and they would declare him a misguided innovator.

If Allāh grants him success in passing this obstacle, then he [the *Shayṭān*] attempts to catch him with the third obstacle, which is the obstacle of major sins. If the *Shayṭān* is successful in overcoming the person in this way, then he will make these sins appear attractive, beautify them in his eyes and convince people to procrastinate over them. He also opens the door to [the innovated] belief that actions are not a part of faith (*irjāʾ*). So the [*Shayṭān*] says to him: 'Faith is merely to believe and it cannot be harmed by actions.' It is possible that he [the *Shayṭān*] causes him to utter a statement that often results in the people's destruction. This is the statement, 'Sins do not harm an individual so long as a person is upon monotheism (*Tawḥīd*) just as good deeds do not benefit the person who is upon polytheism (*Shirk*).' He [the *Shayṭān*] is most pleased if he successfully overcomes the servant with the obstacle of innovation (*bidʿah*) because of the way that it opposes the Religion and since it involves rejection of what Allāh has sent His Messenger (ﷺ) with. Also the one who commits innovation (*bidʿah*) does not repent from it nor does he abandon it and instead he invites the creation to it. [He prefers this] because it necessitates making statements about Allāh without knowledge, it causes hostility towards the clear *Sunnah* and enmity towards the people of the *Sunnah*, and it strives to extinguish the light of the *Sunnah*. It gives leadership to those whom Allāh and His Messenger (ﷺ) have relegated and it discredits those whom Allāh and His Messenger (ﷺ) have given authority. It accepts what is rejected by Allāh and His Messenger (ﷺ) and it rejects what He accepted. It shows allegiance towards the enemies of Allāh and it makes enemies of His allies. It affirms what He negated and negates what He affirmed. It declares the truthful to be liars and the liars to be truthful. It opposes the truth with falsehood and perverts reality so that the truth becomes falsehood and falsehood becomes truth. It incites heresy (*ilḥād*) in the Religion and conceals the truth from the people's hearts. It seeks some deviation in the straight path and opens the door to the changing of the Religion as a whole."[1]

[1] Refer to *Madārij al-Sālikīn* (1/223) by Ibn al-Qayyim.

In light of this fundamental principle, they warn against the books of the people of innovation and misguidance, and they warn against taking from individuals known for innovation (*bidʿah*).

Abū Naṣr ʿUbaydillāh Ibn Saʿīd Ibn Ḥātim al-Wāyilī al-Bakrī as-Sijzī (d.444H) dedicated the eleventh section of his treatise to the people of Zubayd, which was a refutation of those who reject the letter and the voice, to the subject of how we should not loosely give our trust to everyone and take from every book. This is because deception has become prevalent and it has become common for people to ascribe lies to the various schools of thought (*madhāhib*).

He said in this treatise, "Know, may Allāh (ﷻ) have mercy upon us and you, that this section is from the most important sections of this book without question because of the calamities and confusion that has appeared and because of what has been introduced to the people due to their negligence in this matter. This is because the affairs of the people of this time have changed and those who can be truly depended upon are scarce. This is because many people sell their Religion for a lowly price and try to endear themselves to those who are perceived to be large in number! Lies are commonly attributed to the various schools of thought (*madhāhib*). Therefore, it becomes obligatory upon every Muslim who wishes to escape from this to not rely upon everyone and to not depend upon every book. He should not surrender his reins to everyone who outwardly claims to be in agreement with him... Whoever desires safety and security from the likes of these people and to be free of any innovations must make the Book (the *Qurʾān*) and the narration his scale which he uses to measure everything that he sees and hears. If he is knowledgeable concerning these things, he will constantly refer back to them and do so while following the example of the *Salaf*. He should not accept any statement from anyone except that he asks them to provide validation for their claim in the form of a clear verse (of the *Qurʾān*), an established *Sunnah* or a statement of a Companion from a chain of narrators that is authentic. In addition, he should beware of the works of those whose conditions have changed for indeed in these works there are scorpions and perhaps for their venom there is no antidote."[1]

◆◆❖◆◆

[1] Look at some of the *Salafī* principles and points of benefit in the treatise *Risālah al-Imām al-Sijzī ilā Ahl Zubayd fī al-Radd ʿAlā man Ankara al-Ḥarf wa al-Ṣawt* (benefit no. 16), (p. 231-234).

The Ruling Concerning Following The *Salafī* Methodology

You have learned from what has already been mentioned that following the *Salafī* methodology is actually following the Religion which we are obliged to follow due to the command of Allāh and the command of His Messenger (ﷺ).

Muḥammad Ibn al-Ḥusayn al-Ājurrī (d.360H) said, "The intelligent Believer exerts himself to be from the saved sect by following the Book of Allāh (the *Qur'ān*), the *Sunnah* of His Messenger (ﷺ) and the ways of his Companions and their students who followed them in goodness, may the mercy of Allāh be upon them. He follows the statements of the Imāms of the Muslims from those of whom no one is shy to mention, like: Sufyān al-Thawrī (d.167H), al-Awzā'ī (d.157H), Mālik Ibn Anas (d.179H), al-Shāfi'ī (d.204H), Aḥmad Ibn Ḥanbal (d.241H) and Abū 'Ubayd Qāsim Ibn Salām (d.224H) and those who were upon their way from the Scholars of this nation. So whatever they rejected, we reject, and whatever they accepted and stated, we accept and we state. We forsake anything other than that."[1]

Ibn Taymiyyah (d.721H) said, "The knowledge that is legislated and the acts of worship that are legislated [in this Religion] are taken from the Companions of the Messenger of Allāh (ﷺ). As for what has come from those who appeared after them, then it is inappropriate that they are used as a fundamental point of reference even though this person is excused, rather rewarded for their efforts to extract the correct ruling (*ijtihād*) or their efforts to follow another in his ruling (*taqlīd*). Whoever bases his speech in the various Islāmic sciences - whether they are fundamental issues or subsidiary issues - upon the Book (the *Qur'ān*), the *Sunnah* and the narrations that have reached us from the earliest generations, then this individual has traversed upon the path of the Prophet. Similarly, the one who bases his intention, his worship, his deeds and his hearing [of knowledge] as it relates to the fundamental of

[1] Refer to *Kitāb al-Arba'īn Ḥadīthan lil-Ājurrī* with the checking of our distinguished brother Badr al-Badr, published by *Aḍwā' al-Salaf* (1420H).

actions and their subsidiary branches from the affairs of the heart and the actions of the body; whoever bases these things upon true faith, the *Sunnah*, and the guidance of Muḥammad (ﷺ) and his Companions, then he has traversed upon the path of the Prophet. And this is the way of the Imāms of guidance."[1]

◆◆❖◆◆

[1] Refer to *Majmūʿ Fatāwā* (10/362-364) of Ibn Taymiyyah.

The Benefit of Following the *Salafī* Methodology

Whoever follows this methodology acquires many distinct benefits. Some of these are:

1. It is a means of safeguarding oneself from differing.
2. It is a means of eliminating sectarianism.
3. It is a means of guidance which prevents misguidance.
4. Ascribing to it carries the nobility of ascribing oneself to the Prophet (ﷺ).
5. By following this methodology we avoid the various paths of the *Shayṭān*.
6. By following this methodology the Muslims remove themselves from lowliness and disgrace.
7. Applying it helps us to understand the sickness and its cure.
8. Through its application all of the legislation of *Allāh* can be applied.
9. With it an individual can achieve righteousness and good character.
10. With it the Muslims can save themselves from the severe torment of the Fire.
11. Through its implementation the Muslims can enter Paradise.
12. Applying it involves reviving the *Sunnah*.

Any one of these benefits is sufficient by itself to establish the obligation of following this methodology by virtue of the principle that states whatever is required to establish an obligation is an obligation in itself, not to mention the issues of its significance and importance.

At this time, it would be relevant to point out that not everyone who calls himself a *Salafī*, ascribes to the methodology of the people of *Sunnah* and the *Jamāʿah*, or declares himself from the People of *Ḥadīth* should be considered as such until his path and adherence [to the truth] is examined. His affair, condition and speech should be measured in accordance to the Book (the *Qurʾān*), the *Sunnah* and that which was practiced by the Companions and their students who followed them in righteousness. If he conforms to this, then he is from them but if he opposes this then he is not from them. His closeness or remoteness from the straight path depends upon the extent of his opposition [to the truth] and how much he actually conforms to it.

Abū al-Muẓaffar al-Samʿānī (🕮) said, "We have been commanded to follow and we have been encouraged with this. We have been forbidden from innovating (bidʿah) and severely warned against such behavior. The hallmark of the People of the Sunnah is their adherence to the pious predecessors (al-salaf al-ṣāliḥ) and their abandonment of everything that constitutes an innovation (mubtadaʿ) or a matter from the Religion that appears without precedent (muḥdath)."[1]

If this is the case, then what are the characteristics of the Salafī methodology? This will be clarified in the following chapter.

◆ ◆ ❖ ◆ ◆

---

[1] Refer to al-Intiṣār li Ahl al-Ḥadīth by Abū al-Muẓaffar al-Samʿānī by way of the book Ṣawn al-Manṭaq wa al-Kalām (p. 158).

The Second Objective
The Distinct Characteristics of the *Salafī* Methodology

There are distinct characteristics and qualities that the true *Salafī* is known by as opposed to those who falsely claim to adehere to the *Salafī* methodology. From these characteristics is the following:

The First Characteristic: Their allegiance and disassociation (*al-walāʾ wa al-barāʾ*) revolves around following the way of the Messenger (ﷺ).

The Second Characteristic: Their hallmark is that they follow [the *Sunnah*].

The Third Characteristic: They are upon moderation in all of their affairs.

The Fourth Characteristic: They are a people who are united and in agreement, and they are firm and resolute upon the truth.

The Fifth Characteristic: They work towards the establishment of the Religion through the seeking of correct Islāmic knowledge and its application.

Here is a detailed explanation of these characteristics:

◆◆❖◆◆

The First Characteristic Their Allegiance and Disassociation (*al-Walā' wa al-Barā'*) Revolves Around Following the Way Of the Messenger (ﷺ)

According to the *Salafīs*, there is no place for partisanship (*ḥizbiyyah*) that elects an individual, a principle or a book, other than the noble *Qur'ān* and the Prophetic *Sunnah*, as grounds for allegiance and disassociation (*al-walā' wa al-barā'*). Whoever judges the personality that they follow, other than the Messenger (ﷺ), an issue for which there must be allegiance and disassociation (*al-walā' wa al-barā'*) is in reality a person of differing and splitting.

Ibn Taymiyyah (d.728H) said when commenting upon the famous narration concerning the splitting of this nation (*al-iftirāq*), "As for specifying the exact identity of these sects, then indeed several books have been written concerning them and their mention can be found in the books which compile historical accounts of the beliefs and positions [of the various sects]. However, to explicitly state that a particular sect being discussed is one of the seventy two sects requires evidence. This is because Allāh has generally forbidden people from making statements without knowledge, and He has specifically forbidden people from making statements about Him without knowledge. Allāh, the (عزوجل) said,

﴿ قُلْ إِنَّمَا حَرَّمَ رَبِّيَ ٱلْفَوَٰحِشَ مَا ظَهَرَ مِنْهَا وَمَا بَطَنَ وَٱلْإِثْمَ وَٱلْبَغْيَ بِغَيْرِ ٱلْحَقِّ وَأَن تُشْرِكُوا۟ بِٱللَّهِ مَا لَمْ يُنَزِّلْ بِهِۦ سُلْطَٰنًا وَأَن تَقُولُوا۟ عَلَى ٱللَّهِ مَا لَا تَعْلَمُونَ ﴿٣٣﴾ ﴾

> "Say: My Lord has forbidden immorality -what is apparent from it and what remains concealed- and sin and transgression without right and to associate with Allāh that for which He has not sent down any authority and to say concerning Allāh that which you do not know." [Sūrah al-Aʿrāf 7:33]

And Allāh (سبحانه وتعالى) said,

﴿ يَٰٓأَيُّهَا ٱلنَّاسُ كُلُوا۟ مِمَّا فِى ٱلْأَرْضِ حَلَٰلًا طَيِّبًا وَلَا تَتَّبِعُوا۟
خُطُوَٰتِ ٱلشَّيْطَٰنِ ۚ إِنَّهُۥ لَكُمْ عَدُوٌّ مُّبِينٌ ﴿١٦٨﴾ إِنَّمَا يَأْمُرُكُم بِٱلسُّوٓءِ
وَٱلْفَحْشَآءِ وَأَن تَقُولُوا۟ عَلَى ٱللَّهِ مَا لَا تَعْلَمُونَ ﴿١٦٩﴾ ﴾

> "O people, eat from whatever is on earth [that is] permitted to you and do not follow the footsteps of *Shayṭān* (Satan). Indeed, he is to you a clear enemy. He only orders you with evil and immorality and to say concerning Allāh what you do not know."
> [Sūrah al-Baqarah 2:168-169]

And He said,

﴿ وَلَا تَقْفُ مَا لَيْسَ لَكَ بِهِۦ عِلْمٌ ۚ إِنَّ ٱلسَّمْعَ وَٱلْبَصَرَ وَٱلْفُؤَادَ كُلُّ
أُو۟لَٰٓئِكَ كَانَ عَنْهُ مَسْـُٔولًا ﴿٣٦﴾ ﴾

> "And do not pursue things concerning which you have no knowledge. Indeed, the hearing, the sight, and the heart; all of these things are subject to questioning." [Sūrah al-Isrāʾ 17:36]

Likewise, many people speak concerning these sects based solely upon speculation and desires. They proclaim their own group and those who ascribe to the individuals that they follow and show allegiance to it as the people of the *Sunnah* and the *Jamāʿah*, and they declare whoever opposes them to be from the people of innovation (*bidʿah*). This is clear misguidance.

The people who cling to the truth and the *Sunnah* restrict themselves to following the Messenger of Allāh (ﷺ) who,

﴿ وَمَا يَنطِقُ عَنِ ٱلْهَوَىٰٓ ۝٣ إِنْ هُوَ إِلَّا وَحْىٌ يُوحَىٰ ۝٤ ﴾

"He does not speak from his own desires. Rather, it is revelation which is revealed to him."

[Sūrah an-Najm 53:3-4]

He is the only one who must be believed concerning everything that he informs, and he is the only one who must be obeyed in everything that he commands. This station belongs solely to him and should not be given to any of the Imāms. Rather, everyone's statements can be accepted or rejected except for the Messenger of Allāh (ﷺ).

Whoever holds that an individual other than the Messenger of Allāh (ﷺ) can be the criterion by which the people are judged such that those who love this individual and agree with him must be from the people of the *Sunnah* and those who oppose him must be from the people of innovation (*bidʿah*), as is found amongst the various sects that follow the leaders of rhetoric and philosophy (*ʿIlm al-Kalām*) and other than that. Then these individuals are people of innovation (*bidʿah*), misguidance, and division.[1]

---

[1] This would include them [amongst the sects mentioned] in the narration of splitting (*al-iftirāq*). Consequently, they are from the doomed sects that will be destroyed as opposed to the saved sect. It should be noted that this text is from the texts that contain mention of a punishment. This means that the sects that have been threatened with the Hellfire in his statement (ﷺ), "All of them are in the Hellfire except one," then this is their punishment. If Allāh wills He will punish them, and if Allāh wills He may choose to forgive them. As He (ﷻ) said,

→

With this it becomes clear that the people who most deserve to be regarded as "the saved sect" are the People of *Ḥadīth*, the People of the *Sunnah* who do not have a leader to whom they blindly stick except for the Messenger of Allāh (ﷺ). They are the people who are most knowledgeable concerning his statements and actions. They are the people who are most renowned for differentiating between the

---

﴿ إِنَّ ٱللَّهَ لَا يَغْفِرُ أَن يُشْرَكَ بِهِۦ وَيَغْفِرُ مَا دُونَ ذَٰلِكَ لِمَن يَشَآءُ ﴾

"Certainly Allāh does not forgive that partners are associated with Him, but He forgives whatever is less than that for whomever He wills." [Sūrah al-Nisā' 4:48]

Ibn Taymiyyah (d.728H) said in *Majmūʿ Fatāwā* (7/217-218), "In the Book (the *Qur'ān*) and in the *Sunnah*, people who profess Islām are of two types, either believers or hypocrites. The hypocrite will inhabit the lowest station in the Hellfire. As for the believer, then it is possible that he possesses faith that is deficient so he does not qualify for it to be said that he perfected faith; and it is possible for him to possess perfect faith."

Then he went on to say, "What is intended here is that no one should be declared a disbeliever just because he commits a sin or introduces an innovation (*bidʿah*), even if he calls the people to it, unless he is a hypocrite. So if he believed in his heart in the Messenger and what he brought, but he erred in some of his innovated practices due to misconceptions, then this person, in principle, is not a disbeliever. The Kharijites (*Khawārij*) are one of the clearest examples from the people for innovation (*bidʿah*), killing and declaring Muslims to be disbelievers. In spite of this, none of the Companions declared them to be disbelievers, not ʿAlī ibn Abī Ṭālib (رضي الله عنه) or other than him. They judged and treated them the same way as they would treat oppressive and aggressive Muslims...The same applies to the remainder of the seventy-two sects. Whoever from amongst them is a hypocrite is secretly a disbeliever. Whoever is not a hypocrite but is a believer in Allāh and His Messenger (ﷺ) is not considered a disbeliever, even if he errs in understanding something no matter what that mistake. Some of them may possess a branch of hypocrisy which does not condemn a person to the lowest station in the Hellfire. And whoever says that every single one of the seventy-two sects disbelieved with the disbelief that expels an individual from the religion has certainly opposed the Book (the *Qur'ān*) and the *Sunnah*, and the consensus of the Companions (رضي الله عنهم). He has also opposed the consensus of the four Imāms and other than them. For none of them declared all of the seventy-two sects to be disbelievers. Contrary to that, they used to declare some of them to be disbelievers due to specific statements, and this issue has been explained in greater detail elsewhere."

authentic and unauthentic narrations. Their Imāms understand the *Sunnah* correctly, they are well aware of its meanings and adhere to it, believing in it, acting upon it and loving it. They show allegiance to those who embrace it and show animosity to those who reject it. They return ambiguous statements and positions back to what has been revealed concerning it in the Book (the *Qur'ān*) and the *Sunnah*. They do not invent sayings and set it as a fundamental aspect of their religion or a matter to be frequently discussed if it has not been authentically established from the Messenger of Allāh (ﷺ). Contrary to that, they establish whatever the Messenger of Allāh (ﷺ) was sent with from the Book (the *Qur'ān*) and the *Sunnah* as the foundation that they believe in and rely upon."[1]

[1] Refer to *Majmū' Fatāwā* (3/346-347) of Ibn Taymiyyah.

The Second Characteristic
Their Hallmark is That They Follow [the *Sunnah*]

Abū Muḥammad Ibn Abī Zayd al-Qayrawānī (d.386H) said while discussing the affairs of the Religion that the Muslim nation has unanimously agreed upon and the aspects of the *Sunnah* that if opposed is considered innovation (*bid'ah*) and misguidance, "[This requires] total submittance to the *Sunnah*. It is not to be opposed by opinion or averted by way of analogy. The way the texts were interpreted by the righteous *Salaf*, then we interpret them in the same fashion; and whatever way they applied them, then we apply them in the same way and whatever they abandoned then we abandon. We refrain from what they refrained from and we follow them in what they have explained. We imitate them and follow their extrapolations and their opinions concerning the contemporary affairs. We do not leave their *Jamā'ah* [i.e. the opinions of *Salaf*] even in the areas which they differed or explained differently. All of what we have mentioned is the position of the people of *Sunnah* and the Imāms of the people in *fiqh* and *ḥadīth*, as we have clarified. This is also the statement of Imām Mālik."[1]

Abū 'Abdullāh Muḥamad Ibn 'Abdullāh Ibn Abī Zamanayn (d.399H) - رحمه الله - said, "Know, may Allāh have mercy upon you, that the *Sunnah* is the proof that explains the *Qur'ān*, and it is not understood through the use of analogy, nor is it grasped by the intellects. It is only through following the Imāms and the way of the main body of the Muslim nation. Allāh (سبحانه وتعالى) has mentioned a people and praised them when He said,

﴿ فَبَشِّرْ عِبَادِ ﴿١٧﴾ ٱلَّذِينَ يَسْتَمِعُونَ ٱلْقَوْلَ فَيَتَّبِعُونَ أَحْسَنَهُۥٓ ۚ
أُو۟لَٰٓئِكَ ٱلَّذِينَ هَدَىٰهُمُ ٱللَّهُ ۖ وَأُو۟لَٰٓئِكَ هُمْ أُو۟لُوا۟ ٱلْأَلْبَٰبِ ﴿١٨﴾ ﴾

[1] Refer to *al-Jāmi'* (p. 117) of Ibn Abī Zayd al-Qayrawānī.

"So give glad tidings to My servants; [those] who listen to speech and follow the best of it. They are the ones Allāh has guided, and they are people of understanding." [Sūrah az-Zumar 39:17-18]

And He commanded His servants in His statement,

﴿ وَأَنَّ هَـٰذَا صِرَٰطِى مُسْتَقِيمًا فَٱتَّبِعُوهُ وَلَا تَتَّبِعُواْ ٱلسُّبُلَ فَتَفَرَّقَ بِكُمْ عَن سَبِيلِهِ ۚ ذَٰلِكُمْ وَصَّىٰكُم بِهِ لَعَلَّكُمْ تَتَّقُونَ ۝ ﴾

"And certainly, this is My Straight Path, so follow it; and do not follow the [other] paths, for they will divert you from His Way. This is what He has instructed you so that you may become righteous."
[Sūrah al-An'ām 6:153]."[1]

Abū al-Muẓaffar al-Sam'ānī (رحمه الله) said, "We have been commanded to follow and we have been encouraged with this. We have been forbidden from innovating (bid'ah) and severely warned against such behaviour. The hallmark of the People of the Sunnah is their adherence to the pious predecessors (al-salaf al-ṣāliḥ) and their abandonment of everything that constitutes an innovation (mubtada') or a matter from the Religion that appears without precedent (muḥdath)."[2]

The guardian of the Sunnah [Abū al-Qāsim Ismā'īl Ibn Muḥammad] al-Aṣbahānī (d. 535h) - رحمه الله - said, "It is befitting that a man is cautious of newly invented matters, as every newly invented matter [of the Religion] is an innovation (bid'ah). The Sunnah involves believing in the narrations of the Messenger of Allāh (ﷺ) and the abandonment of opposing them with contentious arguments like how and why. Rhetoric

---

[1] Refer to Uṣūl al-Sunnah (p. 35) of Ibn Abī Zamanayn which has been checked and given the title Riyāḍ al-Jannah.
[2] Refer to al-Intiṣār li Ahl al-Ḥadīth of Abū al-Muẓaffar al-Sam'ānī by way of the book Ṣawn al-Manṭaq wa al-Kalām (p. 158).

and argumentation in affairs of the Religion, and pointless debate is considered a newly invented affair, and it can sow the seeds of doubt in the hearts and prevent them from recognizing that which is true and correct. And true knowledge is not demonstrated by the amount of narrations that are transmitted rather true knowledge involves following and practical application. A person should follow the Companions and their students even though they possess a limited amount of knowledge. Whoever opposes the Companions and their students is misguided even if they possess a vast amount of knowledge."[1]

He went on to say, "This is because the affair of the Religion has been clarified for the people so it is upon us to follow since the Religion has come solely from Allāh and is not to be subjected to the intellects of men and their opinions. The Messenger of Allāh (ﷺ) has clarified the *Sunnah* to his nation and explained it to his Companions. So whoever opposes the Companions of the Messenger of Allāh (ﷺ) in any affair from the Religion has certainly gone astray."[2]

They [the *Salafīs*] do not have any secret organization, a president or leader, or an individual that is absolutely followed other than the Messenger (ﷺ). They refer to the Scholars who adhere to the Book (the *Qur'ān*) and the *Sunnah* upon the understanding of the pious predecessors (*al-Salaf al-Ṣāliḥ*).

They have no secret society.

They have no pledge of allegiance

They have no hidden meetings.

They have no undercover hierarchy or anything similar.

---

[1] Refer to *al-Ḥujjah fī Bayān al-Maḥajjah* (2/437-438).
[2] Refer to *al-Ḥujjah fī Bayān al-Maḥajjah* (2/440).

They do not hide anything from the Muslim leaders or from the general Muslim community.

They do not have any secret chains of command, cells or wings.

Rather, they align themselves with the Muslim leaders and the general community of Muslims as has been prescribed in the legislation of Allāh, offering sincere advice inwardly and outwardly.

With this type of behavior they emulate the example of the Companions (ﷺ).

Ibn Taymiyyah (ﷺ) said, "The Imāms of the Muslims like Mālik (d.179H), Ḥammād Ibn Zayd (d.179H), al-Thawrī (d.167H) and others would only speak in unison with the legislation of the Messenger of Allāh (ﷺ), which consists of guidance and healing. Whoever does not possess knowledge of the path of the previous Muslims would substitute that which they were upon with something else, and this is the reason for the appearance of innovation (*bidʿah*) in every nation and the inevitable consequence of this is the disappearance of the *Sunan* [practices] of the Messengers amongst them; and this will result in destruction. That is why they used to say, "Holding fast to the *Sunnah* brings about salvation."

Mālik (ﷺ) said, "The *Sunnah* is like the Ark of Noah (Nūḥ), whoever boards it is saved and whoever abandons it is destroyed." This is the truth. For indeed the Ark of Noah (Nūḥ) was only boarded by those who believed in the Messengers and subsequently followed them, and whoever did not board it disbelieved in the Messengers.

As following the *Sunnah* is following the Message that has come from Allāh, so the one who follows this is like the one who boarded the Ark along with Noah (Nūḥ), both inwardly and outwardly.

The one who decides not to follow the Message is like the one who decided not to join the followers of Noah (Nūḥ) and refused to board the Ark. This is also the case if the Muslim was to ponder over the positions held by the philosophers and the other nations who were upon misguidance and disbelief, they would find that the *Qur'ān* and the *Sunnah* expose their true conditions, clarify their true reality and differentiate between the truth and falsehood of their state.

The Companions were the most knowledgeable of the creation concerning [the Book and the *Sunnah*] just as they were the ones who struggled most against the disbelievers and the hypocrites as ʿAbdullāh Ibn Masʿūd said, 'Whoever from amongst you seeks to take an example, then let him take the example of those who have died. Indeed those who are living are not immune from *fitnah* [trial and temptation]. Those were the Companions of Muḥammad; they were those from this nation that possessed the purest hearts, the greatest level of knowledge and they were the least excessive. They are people whom Allāh specifically chose to be Companions of His Prophet and those who would establish His Religion. So recognize their rights and cling to their guidance for indeed they were upon the guidance of the Straight Path.'"[1]

◆◆❖◆◆

[1] Refer to *Majmūʿ Fatāwā* (4/137) of Ibn Taymiyyah.

The Third Characteristic
They are Upon Moderation in All of Their Affairs

From the distinct characteristics of Islām is moderation and balance.[1]

---

[1] Refer to *al-Islām Maqāṣiduhu wa Khaṣā'iṣuhu* (p. 50) by Dr. Muḥammad al-ʿAqlah. Shaykhul-Islām Ibn Taymiyyah (ﷺ) says in *al-Jawāb al-Ṣaḥīḥ* (1/6-8), "Indeed, Allāh (ﷻ) honoured Prophet Muḥammad (ﷺ) with specific characteristics that distinguish him from all of the Prophets and Messengers, and He endowed him with both a law and a methodology. It is the most superior law and most complete and clearest methodology. Likewise, He made the nation of Muḥammad the best nation that has arisen from mankind. They surpass seventy nations and they are the best of them and most noble to Allāh. Allāh guided them with His Book (the *Qur'ān*) and His Messenger (ﷺ) to the truth of the affairs in which the people which preceded them differed. He made them a nation of moderation, fairness and excellence. They are moderate concerning the *Tawḥīd* of Allāh and His Names and Attributes. They are moderate in their beliefs concerning His Messengers, His Books, and the laws of His Religion, that which is commanded and forbidden and that which is lawful and unlawful. So He commanded them with good and forbade them from evil and made lawful for them the good and beneficial things and forbade them from the lowly and harmful things. He did not forbid them from anything that is good and beneficial like that which was forbidden from the Jews. He did not make lawful anything from the lowly and harmful things like that which was made permissible by the Christians. He did not place as many restrictions upon them in issues relating to purification and impurities as He did with the Jews. Nor did He completely eliminate the issue of purification and impurities as the Christians did such that they do not require that an individual purifies himself from sexual impurity, perform ablution for the Prayer or avoid impurities when praying. In fact, many of their worshippers view the use of impurities as a means of devoutness and obedience. To the extent that it is said concerning the praiseworthy characteristics of an ascetic monk that, 'He has not touched [i.e. bathed] water in 40 years.' This is the very reason they have abandoned circumcision even though it was from the legislation of Abraham al-Khaleel (عليه السلام) and his followers. And with the Jews, if a woman menstruates, then they do not eat or drink with her nor do they remain with her in the same house. As for the Christians, then they do not prohibit sexual intercourse with a woman who is menstruating. The Jews do not believe that it is compulsory to remove impurities. If some impurity were to touch the garment of one of them they would cut it out with scissors. According to the Christians nothing is considered unlawful to eat or impermissible to wear while in a state of prayer. The Muslims are also moderate in matters of legislation. They do not reject a ruling established by an →

abrogating text due to the presence of a ruling established by an abrogated text as the Jews did. They do not change any of the clear legislation nor innovate a new legislation that Allāh has not permitted as the Christians did. They do not exaggerate the station of the Prophets and the righteous as do the Christians nor do they deprive them of their appropriate status like the Jews. They do not describe the Creator with the deficiencies and imperfections of the creation like poverty, miserliness or inability as did the Jews. They do not describe the creation with the characteristics of the Creator, as did the Christians, since there is nothing like unto Him. They are not too proud to worship Him as are the Jews and they do not commit *Shirk* when they worship Him as do the Christians. Certainly, the people of the *Sunnah* in Islām are like the people of Islām when compared with the people of other religions. They are moderate concerning the attributes of Allāh (ﷻ) as they take the middle path that falls between the people who reject or deny them and the people who resemble His Attributes to that of the creation or make comparisons for them. They only describe Allāh in the manner in which He has described Himself and in the way that His Messengers described Him without negation or making examples. In such a way that His attributes of perfection are affirmed and to declare Him free of equals or partners. They affirm [His Attributes] without likening them to the creation and they negate [imperfections] without denying [His Attributes]. As He (ﷻ) said, "**And there is nothing like unto Him...**" which is a refutation of those who compare Him to His creation. And His statement, "**And He is the All-Hearing, All-Seeing...**" is a refutation of those who deny His Attributes. He says, "**Say: He is Allāh; the One. Allāh the Eternal Provider; He does not beget nor was He begotten, and there is not for Him any equal.**" So al-Ṣamad here or the Eternal Provider is the absolute independent sovereign who possesses the Attributes of perfection. And al-Aḥad or the One is the One who possesses no equal and has no example. They [the People of *Sunnah*] are also moderate concerning the issue of Allāh's actions. They take the middle path which falls between the *Muʿtazilah* who deny *al-Qadr* and the *Jabariyyah* who negate the wisdom of Allāh, His mercy, His justice, and ultimately use *Qadr* (the Divine Decree) as an excuse to rebel against Allāh's commands and threats, and His rewards and punishments. In the issue of the [texts that contain] promises [of Paradise] and threats [of the Hellfire], [the people of *Sunnah* take the middle path which falls] between the *Waʿīdiyyah* who say that the sinful Muslims will remain in the Hellfire forever and the *Murjiʾah* who reject some of the textual threats and the superiority that Allāh has given to the righteous servants over the wicked sinners. They are also moderate concerning the issue of the Companions of the Messenger of Allāh (ﷺ). [They take the middle path] between those who exaggerate concerning some of them, claiming for them divinity, prophethood or infallibility, and those who are negligent concerning them like those who declare some of them to be disbelievers or sinners. The companions are without doubt the best of this nation."

Moderation is from the most distinguishing characteristics of the Religion [Islam]. Allāh (ﷻ) said,

﴿ ٱهْدِنَا ٱلصِّرَٰطَ ٱلْمُسْتَقِيمَ ۝٦ صِرَٰطَ ٱلَّذِينَ أَنْعَمْتَ عَلَيْهِمْ غَيْرِ ٱلْمَغْضُوبِ عَلَيْهِمْ وَلَا ٱلضَّآلِّينَ ۝٧ ﴾

"Guide us to the straight path. The path of those upon whom You have shown Your favor. Not those with whom You are angered or those who are astray."
[Sūrah al-Fātiḥah 1: 6-7]

This is cited as an evidence here because He (ﷻ) described the Straight Path as other than the path of those whom He is angry with, which is a reference to the Jews who were excessive in their religion, and not the path of the Christians who were excessive in their worship and asceticism to the point that they exceeded the limits of their legislation. Their excessiveness was not restricted to their worship but they even exceeded the limits in matters of belief as Allāh (ﷻ) said,

﴿ يَٰٓأَهْلَ ٱلْكِتَٰبِ لَا تَغْلُوا۟ فِى دِينِكُمْ وَلَا تَقُولُوا۟ عَلَى ٱللَّهِ إِلَّا ٱلْحَقَّ ۚ إِنَّمَا ٱلْمَسِيحُ عِيسَى ٱبْنُ مَرْيَمَ رَسُولُ ٱللَّهِ وَكَلِمَتُهُۥٓ أَلْقَىٰهَآ إِلَىٰ مَرْيَمَ وَرُوحٌ مِّنْهُ ۖ فَـَٔامِنُوا۟ بِٱللَّهِ وَرُسُلِهِۦ ۖ وَلَا تَقُولُوا۟ ثَلَٰثَةٌ ۚ ٱنتَهُوا۟ خَيْرًا لَّكُمْ ۚ إِنَّمَا ٱللَّهُ إِلَٰهٌ وَٰحِدٌ ۖ سُبْحَٰنَهُۥٓ أَن يَكُونَ لَهُۥ وَلَدٌ ۘ لَّهُۥ مَا فِى ٱلسَّمَٰوَٰتِ وَمَا فِى ٱلْأَرْضِ ۗ وَكَفَىٰ بِٱللَّهِ وَكِيلًا ۝١٧١ ﴾

"O People of the Scripture, do not commit excess in your religion or say about Allāh except the truth. The Messiah, Jesus, the son of Mary, was but a Messenger of Allāh and His word which He directed to Mary and a soul (created at a command) **from Him. So believe in Allāh and His Messengers. And do not say, "Three"; desist - it is better for you. Indeed, Allāh is but one God. Exalted is He above having a son. To Him belongs whatever is in the heavens and whatever is on the earth. And sufficient is Allāh as Disposer of affairs."** [Sūrah al-Nisā' 4:171]

If the Straight Path is a path other than that of the Jews and the Christians and the path of the Jews and the Christians was a path of excessiveness [as explained above], then this indicates that the straight path is a path that allows no excessiveness. Therefore, it falls between the two extremes of excessiveness and negligence. This is the meaning of moderation that is the methodology of the Religion of Islām.

It has been transmitted upon the authority of ʿAbdullāh Ibn Masʿūd that he said, "The Messenger of Allāh (ﷺ) drew a straight line. Then he said, 'This is the path of Allāh.' Then he drew other lines on the right and left of it. Then he said, 'These are different paths. On each one of these paths is a *Shayṭān* [devil] calling to it.' Then he recited,

﴿ وَأَنَّ هَٰذَا صِرَٰطِي مُسۡتَقِيمٗا فَٱتَّبِعُوهُۖ وَلَا تَتَّبِعُواْ ٱلسُّبُلَ فَتَفَرَّقَ بِكُمۡ عَن سَبِيلِهِۦۚ ﴾

"And certainly, this is My Straight Path, so follow it; and do not follow the [other] **paths, for they will divert you from His way."** [Sūrah al-Anʿām 6:153]."[1]

---

[1] Related by Aḥmad in the *Musnad* (1/435,465), al-Dārimī in the introduction his *Sunan*, Ibn Abū ʿĀṣim in *al-Sunnah* (1/13), Ibn Ḥibbān (*al-Iḥsān*, 1/180-181, no. 6-7) and al-Ḥākim in his *Mustadrak* (2/318). It was also related upon the authority of →

The Straight Path necessitates that this is a path of moderation and excellence, which exists between the two extremes of excessiveness and negligence.

It has been transmitted upon the authority of Ibn ʿAbbās that he said, "It was said to the Messenger of Allāh (ﷺ), "Which of the previous legislations is most beloved to Allāh?" To this he replied, "The easy and tolerant Religion of Islāmic monotheism (*al-Ḥanīfiyyah al-Samḥah*)."[1]

This narration provides textual evidence that Islām is an easy and tolerant Religion [*al-Ḥanīfiyyah al-Samḥah*]. The attribute of [*al-Samāḥah*] easiness and tolerance totally negates excessiveness and harshness.

Ibn Taymiyyah (ﷺ) said concerning the People of *Sunnah* and the *Jamāʿah*, "Likewise concerning the remaining issues of the *Sunnah*, they are moderate because they adhere to the Book of Allāh and the *Sunnah* of His Messenger (ﷺ) and what was agreed upon by the first generation from the *Muhājirūn* (those who migrated from Makkah to Madīnah) and the *Anṣār* (the inhabitants of Madīnah who welcomed the Prophet and his Companions) and those who followed them upon goodness."[2]

Jābir Ibn ʿAbdullāh (ﷺ) by Ibn Mājah (no. 11) and in Ibn Abū ʿĀṣim in Kitāb *al-Sunnah* (1/13). This *ḥadīth* was authenticated by Ibn Ḥibbān and al-Ḥākim. The person that checked the book, *al-Iḥsān*, declared it to be sound, and Shaykh al-Albānī declared it to be *Ṣaḥīḥ li ghayrihi* (Ṣaḥīḥ due other narrations) in *Ẓilāl al-Jannah* (1/13).

[1] Related by Aḥmad in the *Musnad* (*al-Risālah*, 4/17, no. 2107), al-Bukhārī in *al-Adab al-Mufrad* (*Ṣaḥīḥ al-Adab al-Mufrad*, p. 122, no. 220/287) and ʿAbd Ibn Ḥumayd in his *Musnad* (*al-Muntakhab*, 1/497, no. 567). It was also mentioned by al-Bukhārī in *ta'leeq* form in *Kitāb al-Īmān* in the chapter concerning the easiness of the Religion and the statement, "The most beloved Religion to Allāh is *al-Ḥanīfiyyah al-Samḥah*." Ibn Ḥajar declared the chain of narration for this *ḥadīth* to be *Ḥasan* in *Fatḥ al-Bārī* (1/94). Shaykh al-Albānī declared this narration to be *Ḥasan li ghayrihi* (*Ḥasan* due other narrations) in *Ṣaḥīḥ al-Adab al-Mufrad* and also in *Silsilah al-Aḥādīth al-Ṣaḥīḥah* (no. 881) and the checker of *al-Muntakhab* also declared this narration *Ḥasan li ghayrihi* (*Ḥasan* due other narrations); and the checkers of the *Musnad* declared this narration to be *Ṣaḥīḥ li ghayrihi* (*Ṣaḥīḥ* due other narrations).

[2] Refer to *Majmūʿ Fatāwā* (3/375) of Ibn Taymiyyah.

[The *Salafīs*] are not extreme or harsh.

They do not permit roughness or dissonance.

They do not bring forth reasons and excuses to justify a lack of submittance and surrender.

Ibn Qayyim al-Jawziyyah (d.751H) – رحمه الله - said, "The difference between being moderate (*iqtiṣād*) and being negligent (*taqṣīr*) is that moderation (*iqtiṣād*) is positioned between the two extremes of excessiveness and negligence. Moderation is opposed by two conflicting extremes: Negligence (*taqṣīr*) and going beyond bounds (*mujāwazah*). So the one who is considered moderate (*al-muqtaṣid*) takes the balanced and middle course, and abandons the conflicting extremes.

Allāh (سبحانه وتعالى) said,

﴿ وَٱلَّذِينَ إِذَآ أَنفَقُواْ لَمۡ يُسۡرِفُواْ وَلَمۡ يَقۡتُرُواْ وَكَانَ بَيۡنَ ذَٰلِكَ قَوَامٗا ٦٧ ﴾

"And those who when they give of their wealth; they neither spend extravagantly nor miserly, but they maintain a consistent manner between those extremes." [Sūrah al-Furqān 25:67]

And Allāh (سبحانه وتعالى) said,

﴿ وَلَا تَجۡعَلۡ يَدَكَ مَغۡلُولَةً إِلَىٰ عُنُقِكَ وَلَا تَبۡسُطۡهَا كُلَّ ٱلۡبَسۡطِ ﴾

"And do not allow your hand to be bound to your neck [like a miser] **or completely extend it** [like a spendthrift]**."** [Sūrah al-Isrāʾ 17:29]

And Allāh (سبحانه وتعالى) says,

﴿ وَكُلُوا۟ وَٱشْرَبُوا۟ وَلَا تُسْرِفُوٓا۟ ﴾

"And eat and drink but be not excessive."

[Sūrah al-Aʿrāf 7:31]

All aspects of the Religion exist between these two extremes. Actually, Islām is the moderate Religion when compared to other religions, and the *Sunnah* is an example of moderation in the midst of innovation (*bidʿah*). The Religion of Allāh exists between the extremes of those who are excessive and the negligence of those who are negligent.

This is also the case with interpretive jurisprudence (*ijtihād*) which involves the exertion of great efforts in order to arrive at the truth. And excessiveness involves transgressing this point and overstepping its limits.

Allāh has not commanded a matter except that the *Shayṭān* attempts to misguide the people with his whispering in two ways, either through excessiveness and transgression, or through heedlessness and negligence. These are two sources of evil that cannot be completely prevented from corrupting the beliefs, intentions and actions except for the one who walks in the footsteps of the Messenger of Allāh (ﷺ) and abandons the statements of the people and their opinions in favour of what he came with; and not the one who abandons what he came with in favour of the statements of the people and their opinions.

These two dangerous diseases have overpowered most of the children of Ādam. This is why the *Salaf* used to warn in the most severe manner from these two diseases, and they would frighten those who succumb to either of these maladies with destruction. Indeed, these two characteristics sometimes combine in a single person as is the case in most of the creation so an inidivual could be negligent with some aspects of his Religion and excessive and extreme in others. The one who is guided is the one whom Allāh guides."[1]

---

[1] Refer to *al-Rūḥ* (p. 347) of Ibn al-Qayyim.

In keeping with this characteristic, those who ascribe to *Salafiyyah* reject harshness, extremism and excessiveness.

Al-Ghulūw [extremism] is to go to extremes in a particular issue and be harsh by transgressing the set boundaries. This incorporates the meaning of exaggeration.[1] It is said: (*ghalā fī al-shay'*) He was excessive or extreme in something [in the past tense], (*yaghlū*) he is excessive or extreme [in the present tense], and (*ghulūwan*) which means extremism. It is said that the price *ghalā* which basically means that the normal asking price has been exceeded. It is said the shares *yaghlū ghalwan* with ghalwan taking a *fatḥah* then a *sukūn*, when it reaches the highest possible price hoped for.

In the narration of Ibn ʿAbbās (☼) he says, "The Messenger of Allāh (ﷺ) said to me on the morning of ʿAqabah while he was on his mount, 'Could you gather for me some small pebbles?' So I gathered for him some pebbles that would be like the stones that are flicked with the finger, and I placed them in his hand. He said, '[Throw] the ones like these. And beware of going to extremes in matters of the Religion, for indeed those who came before you were destroyed because they went to extremes in matters of the Religion.'"[2]

It has been transmitted upon the authority of Anas ibn Mālik (☼) that the Prophet (ﷺ) said, "Make things easy for the people and do not make things difficult, and give glad tidings and do not chase them away. For indeed you were only sent to make things easy and you were not sent to make things difficult."[3]

---

[1] The Arabic word *taʿammuq* means to exhibit harshness in a matter to a level where the justified limits are exceeded. Refer to *Fatḥ al-Bārī* (13/278).
[2] Related by Aḥmad in the *Musnad* (*al-Risālah*, 3/351, no. 1851), al-Nisāʾī (no. 3057), Ibn Mājah (no. 3029), Ibn Khuzaymah (4/274, no. 2867), Ibn Ḥibbān (*al-Iḥsān*, 9/183, no. 3871) and al-Ḥākim (1/466). The *ḥadīth* was authenticated by Ibn Khuzaymah, Ibn Ḥibbān, and al-Ḥākim and its chain of narration was declared *Ṣaḥīḥ* by those who checked the *Musnad* of Imām Aḥmad and by the one who checked *al-Iḥsān*.
[3] Related by al-Bukhārī (no. 69) and Muslim (no. 1734).

It has also been transmitted upon the authority of ʿAbdullāh Ibn Masʿūd (🙵) that he (🙵) said, "The *mutanaṭṭiʿūn* [those who go to extremes] are ruined. The *mutanaṭṭiʿūn* are ruined. The *mutanaṭṭiʿūn* are ruined."[1]

The *mutanaṭṭiʿūn* mentioned in this *ḥadīth*, as the explainers of this narration have mentioned, are those who delve too deeply, go to extremes and transgress the set limits in their statements and actions.

This narration apparently describes the condition of the *mutanaṭṭiʿūn* while it also signifies the prohibition of excessiveness.

◆ ◆ ❖ ◆ ◆

---

[1] Related by Muslim (no. 2670).

The Fourth Characteristic
They are a People who are United and in Agreement, and They are Firm and Resolute upon the Truth

The *Salafīs* seek to preserve and strengthen the *Jamāʿah* [community of Muslims] and banish dissention, but the type of Jamāʿah that they want to unite upon is what the Messenger of Allāh (ﷺ) was upon and his Companions.

Abū al-Muẓaffar al-Samʿānī (رحمه الله) said, "From what shows that the people of *ḥadīth* are upon the truth is that if you were to examine all of their written works from the first of them to the last of them, from the oldest of them to the newest of them, despite them living in different lands and during different times, and the great distances that separate them and the fact that each one of them inhabited a different region, you will find them when expounding upon their beliefs upon a single way, upon a single method and they traverse upon a single path without deviating from it or turning away from it. They are united in their speech concerning it, and their actions are one. You will not witness any differing and separation amongst them about anything, even if it is insignificant. Rather, if you were to collect everything that has been stated upon their tongues and what they conveyed from their predecessors, you will find that it is as if it has come from a single heart and come from a single tongue. And is there any evidence for truth that is clearer than this?

Allāh (سبحانه وتعالى) says,

﴿ أَفَلَا يَتَدَبَّرُونَ ٱلْقُرْءَانَ ۚ وَلَوْ كَانَ مِنْ عِندِ غَيْرِ ٱللَّهِ لَوَجَدُوا۟ فِيهِ
ٱخْتِلَٰفًا كَثِيرًا ﴿٨٢﴾ ﴾

"Do they not reflect upon the *Qur'ān*? Had it been from other than Allāh, then they would have found therein much contradiction." [Sūrah al-Nisāʾ 4:82]

And Allāh (ﷻ) says,

﴿ وَٱعۡتَصِمُواْ بِحَبۡلِ ٱللَّهِ جَمِيعٗا وَلَا تَفَرَّقُواْۚ وَٱذۡكُرُواْ نِعۡمَتَ ٱللَّهِ عَلَيۡكُمۡ إِذۡ كُنتُمۡ أَعۡدَآءٗ فَأَلَّفَ بَيۡنَ قُلُوبِكُمۡ فَأَصۡبَحۡتُم بِنِعۡمَتِهِۦٓ إِخۡوَٰنٗا وَكُنتُمۡ عَلَىٰ شَفَا حُفۡرَةٖ مِّنَ ٱلنَّارِ فَأَنقَذَكُم مِّنۡهَاۗ كَذَٰلِكَ يُبَيِّنُ ٱللَّهُ لَكُمۡ ءَايَٰتِهِۦ لَعَلَّكُمۡ تَهۡتَدُونَ ١٠٣ ﴾

> **"And hold firmly to the rope of Allāh all together and do not be divided. And remember the favour of Allāh upon you -when you were enemies He brought your hearts together and you became, by His mercy, brothers. And you were on the edge of a pit of the fire, and He saved you from it. Thus does Allāh make clear to you His *āyāt* that you may be guided."**
>
> [Sūrah Āli-ʿImrān 3:103]

But if you were to look at the people of desires and innovation (*bidʿah*) you would see that they are divided and differ with one another; they are factions and sects. It would be unlikely to find two groups from among them that are upon the same path in terms of their beliefs. Some of them declare others amongst them to be innovators (*mubtadiʿūn*), and some of them go further and make *takfīr* [declare a Muslim to be a disbeliever]. The son declares his father to be a disbeliever, a man declares his brother to be a disbeliever, and the neighbor declares his neighbor to be a disbeliever. You will always find them disputing, hating and differing with one another. Their entire lives have passed them by and their words are still not in agreement. You may believe that they are together but their hearts are divided. This is because they are a people who do not understand.

Have not you heard about the *Muʿtazilah*, even though they share this ascription and nickname the *Muʿtazilah* from Baghdād declare the *Muʿtazilah* from al-Baṣrah to be disbelievers. The companions of Abū ʿAlī al-Jubā'ī declare his son Abū Hāshim to be a disbeliever and the supporters of Abū Hāshim declare his father, Abū ʿAlī to be a disbeliever.

The same applies to the rest of their figureheads and those who have formulated certain position from amongst them. If you were to reflect upon their statements, you would see that they are divided, they declare one another to be disbelievers and they renounce one another.

This is also the case with the Kharijites (*Khawārij*) and the *Rawāfiḍ* and how they interact with one another. The rest of the people of innovation (*mubtadiʿūn*) resemble them in this. Is there any evidence for falsehood clearer than this?!

And Allāh (ﷻ) says,

﴿ إِنَّ ٱلَّذِينَ فَرَّقُواْ دِينَهُمْ وَكَانُواْ شِيَعًا لَّسْتَ مِنْهُمْ فِي شَيْءٍ ۚ إِنَّمَآ أَمْرُهُمْ إِلَى ٱللَّهِ ﴾

> **"Indeed, those who have divided their religion and split off into sects; you should not concern yourself with them in the least** [O Muḥammad]**. Their affair is exclusively for Allāh."** [Sūrah al-Anʿām 6:159]

The reason behind the unity of the people of *ḥadīth* is that they take their Religion from the Book (the *Qur'ān*) and the *Sunnah*, and they rely upon that which is transmitted. This has left them in agreement and harmony. Whereas the people of innovation (*mubtadiʿūn*) have taken their Religion from logic and theoretical opinion so this has left them to inherit division and differing. As for the narrations and transmissions conveyed by trustworthy and reliable individuals then they rarely differ and even if they differ about a word or phrase then this type of differing does not harm the Religion or spoil it.

However, as for the arguments that are derived from the intellect then they rarely agree. In fact, the intellect of each individual interprets things differently than the next person and this is very clear, and all praise is due to Allāh. With this the difference should be understood between differing amongst the schools of thought (*madhāhib*) in the branch issues of the Religion as opposed to differing in the fundamental issues of belief.

We found that the Companions of the Messenger of Allāh (ﷺ) used to differ, [after the death of the Prophet], in issues of jurisprudence but this did not prompt splitting or sectarianism. This was because they never departed from the [teachings] of the Religion and they only differed in areas where disagreement was allowed [through interpretive jurisprudence (*ijtihād*) in order to arrive at an informed opinion and in order to extract rulings from the Book (the *Qurʾān*) and the *Sunnah* regarding the issues that were not explicitly addressed with a text]. They held different statements and opinions in many issues...Which would require a great length to enumerate upon from the matters of commerce, marriage and divorce; and also in a multitude of other issues related to purification, the way Prayer should be performed and the other acts of worship. With this type of differing in these affairs they were still worthy of praise; and this form of differing is a mercy from Allāh upon this nation since He aided them with certainty. Then the Scholars thoroughly researched those issues where they did not find its legal ruling in the *Qurʾān* and the *Sunnah*. So even though they differed in these things they were a people who loved one another and offered sincere advice. The brotherhood of Islām remained and they did not cease to be in a state of harmony.

When these ignoble desires appeared which direct its proponent towards the Hellfire enmity appeared and the people split and became sects. The brotherhood of the Religion became severed and the harmony ceased. This proves that this type of splitting and division occurred as a result of innovations introduced by *Shayṭān*, which he placed in the mouths of his allies to cause them to differ and provoke them to declare one another to be disbelievers.

Every issue that arose in Islām and the people disputed regarding it and differed but these differences did not incite enmity, animosity or division between them and there was a continuance in the harmony, sincere advice, love, mercy and compassion, then these are from the issues of Islām in which research and scrutiny is permitted. Adopting any of these positions does not justify *takfīr* (the person being declared a disbeliever) or *tabdī'* (being declared an innovator) since this type of differing existed between the Companions and their students, and the harmony and love was maintained.

Conversely, every issue that appears and which the people differ about and this differing leads to taking sides, shunning, boycotting, severing relationships and possibly even escalates to *takfīr*, then you know that this is in no way related to the religion. It is obligatory upon every individual of sound mind to distance himself from this and avoid indulging into disputes of this nature because Allāh has stipulated that as a result of our implementation of Islām that we become brothers."[1]

And Allāh (ﷻ) said,

﴿ وَٱذْكُرُوا۟ نِعْمَتَ ٱللَّهِ عَلَيْكُمْ إِذْ كُنتُمْ أَعْدَآءً فَأَلَّفَ بَيْنَ قُلُوبِكُمْ فَأَصْبَحْتُم بِنِعْمَتِهِۦٓ إِخْوَٰنًا ﴾

"And remember the favour of Allāh upon you - when you were enemies He brought your hearts together and you became, by His mercy, brothers."

[Sūrah Āli-'Imrān 3:103]

---

[1] Refer to *al-Intiṣār li Ahl al-Ḥadīth* by way of the book *Ṣawn al-Manṭaq wal-Kalām* (p. 165-169). Compare this to what is written in *al-I'tiṣām* (2/231-233) where much of this section has been summarized but he did not attribute it to Abū al-Muẓaffar al-Sam'ānī. Instead, he said, "Some scholars have said," and then he summarized this, quoting the main objectives.

Ibn Taymiyyah (ﷺ) said, "You will definitely find that those who change their positions the most are the people of rhetoric (*ahl al-kalām*), and they are those most famous for asserting a position in one place and then resolutely promoting its opposite in another place and declaring the one who holds the first position to be a disbeliever. This is a proof of their lack of certainty. For indeed faith is as Heraclius said when he asked Abū Sufyān about those who embraced Islām and joined the Prophet (ﷺ), 'Do any of them abandon their Religion because they are discontented with it after having entered into it?' He replied, 'No.' Then he [Heraclius] said, 'This is the nature of faith. When its joy enters into the heart no one becomes displeased with it.'[1]

Based on this, some of the *Salaf* like ʿUmar Ibn ʿAbdul-ʿAzīz or other than him stated, "Whoever allows his Religion to become a matter of debate will frequently change."

As for the people of the *Sunnah* and *ḥadīth*, then it is not known that a single one of their Scholars or even one of their righteous laypeople ever withdrew their position and retracted their beliefs. They are the most patient of the people upon their beliefs even if they are made to endure all kinds of trials and tribulations. This is the condition of the Prophets and their followers from those who have preceded us like the people of the trench and the like of them. This was the case with the *Salaf* of this nation from the Companions and their students and other than them from the Imāms. To the extent that Imām Mālik used to say, "Do not envy anyone who has not been subjected to severe affliction in this affair." He would say, "Indeed, Allāh must test the Believer with trials and affliction. Then, if he is patient, his level increases."

---

[1] Related by al-Bukhārī (no, 7) upon the authority of ʿAbdullāh ibn ʿAbbās (ﷺ) and a shorter version (no. 51) with the wording: Upon the authority of ʿAbdullāh Ibn ʿAbbās who said: Abū Sufyān Ibn Ḥarb informed me that Heraclius said to him: I asked you are they (the followers of Muhammad) increasing or decreasing in number. And you replied that they are increasing. This is the way of true faith until it is complete. I asked you whether any of them became displeased and forsook their Religion. Then you replied: No. This is the nature of faith. When its joy enters into the heart and mixes with it, no one becomes displeased with it.

As Allāh (ﷻ) said,

﴿ الٓمٓ ۝١ أَحَسِبَ ٱلنَّاسُ أَن يُتۡرَكُوٓاْ أَن يَقُولُوٓاْ ءَامَنَّا وَهُمۡ لَا
يُفۡتَنُونَ ۝٢ وَلَقَدۡ فَتَنَّا ٱلَّذِينَ مِن قَبۡلِهِمۡۖ فَلَيَعۡلَمَنَّ ٱللَّهُ ٱلَّذِينَ
صَدَقُواْ وَلَيَعۡلَمَنَّ ٱلۡكَٰذِبِينَ ۝٣ ﴾

"Alif, Lām, Mīm. Do the people think that they will be left to say, 'We believe,' and they will not be tested? Surely, We have tried those who came before them, and certainly Allāh will clearly identify those who are truthful, and certainly He will clearly identify the liars." [Sūrah al-ʿAnkabūt 29:1-3]

And Allāh (ﷻ) said,

﴿ وَجَعَلۡنَا مِنۡهُمۡ أَئِمَّةً يَهۡدُونَ بِأَمۡرِنَا لَمَّا صَبَرُواْۖ وَكَانُواْ
بِـَٔايَٰتِنَا يُوقِنُونَ ۝٢٤ ﴾

"And We established from amongst them, leaders who would guide in accordance with Our command when they were patient and used to be certain of Our signs." [Sūrah al-Sajdah 32:24]

And Allāh (ﷻ) said,

﴿ وَٱلۡعَصۡرِ ۝١ إِنَّ ٱلۡإِنسَٰنَ لَفِي خُسۡرٍ ۝٢ إِلَّا ٱلَّذِينَ ءَامَنُواْ وَعَمِلُواْ
ٱلصَّٰلِحَٰتِ وَتَوَاصَوۡاْ بِٱلۡحَقِّ وَتَوَاصَوۡاْ بِٱلصَّبۡرِ ۝٣ ﴾

> **"By the time, truly, mankind is in loss, except those who believe and do righteous deeds, and advise one another with truth, and advise one another with patience."** [Sūrah al-ʿAsr 103: 1-3]

Those who remain steadfast upon their positions from the people of desires, then this is due to the elements of truth that they adhere to as there must be with every innovation (*bidʿah*) that is practised by a large group of people some element of truth which they hold onto that the Messenger (ﷺ) came with and with which the people of the *Sunnah* and *ḥadīth* agree, which causes it to be accepted. This is because pure falsehood will not be accepted under any circumstances.

In summary, firmness and steadfastness among the people of *ḥadīth* and the *Sunnah* is far more common and prevalent than what you find among the people of rhetoric (*ahl al-kalām*) and philosophy. In fact, the philosophers are more indecisive and uncertain than the people of rhetoric (*ahl al-kalām*). This is because the people of rhetoric (*ahl al-kalām*) possess an amount of truth which they have acquired from the Prophets that is not present among the philosophers. For this reason you'll find that Abū al-Ḥusayn al-Baṣrī and the like of him displayed more conviction than Ibn Sīnā and the like of him.

You will also find that the people of philosophy and rhetoric (*ahl al-kalām*) are the people that divide and differ the most and each one of them claim that their statement is the definitive truth which is supported by evidence. The people of the *Sunnah* and *ḥadīth* are the people with the greatest unity and harmony. The closer the sect is to them, then the closer they will be to unity and harmony. For example, the *Muʿtazilah* experience more harmony and agreement than the philosophers since the philosophers have so many contradictory positions that only Allāh can keep count of them. They have different positions concerning affairs of divinity, the resurrection, prophethood, and even in the natural sciences, mathematics and astrology.

Those who have compiled books documenting the positions and statements of the earlier generations [of philophers] like Abū al-Ḥasan al-Ashʿarī (d.324H) in his book, *al-Maqālāt*, and al-Qāḍī Abū Bakr in the book, *al-Daqā'iq min Maqālātihim*, have cited exponentially more than what has just been mentioned by al-Farābī, Ibn Sīnā and those who are similar to them..."[1]

Thus, the *Salafīs* do not fall into blameworthy differing that is a characteristic of weakness.

A person cannot protect himself from falling into this except by obeying Allāh and obeying the Messenger (ﷺ).

Allāh (ﷻ) said,

﴿ وَأَطِيعُوا۟ ٱللَّهَ وَرَسُولَهُۥ وَلَا تَنَـٰزَعُوا۟ فَتَفْشَلُوا۟ وَتَذْهَبَ رِيحُكُمْ ۖ وَٱصْبِرُوٓا۟ ۚ إِنَّ ٱللَّهَ مَعَ ٱلصَّـٰبِرِينَ ﴿٤٦﴾ ﴾

"And obey Allāh and His Messenger and do not dispute, lest you lose courage and your strength may depart; and be patient. Indeed, Allāh is with the patient."

[Sūrah al-Anfāl 8:46]

When the *Sunnah* is followed, implemented and understood in the same manner as the pious predecessors (*al-Salaf al-Ṣāliḥ*), then this is obedience to Allāh and His Messenger (ﷺ). This is the path to safely escape blameworthy differing.

Al-Tirmidhī collected the following narration in his *Sunan* in the book of knowledge (*Kitāb al-'Ilm*) within the chapter, 'What has been narrated concerning adherence to the *Sunnah* and avoiding religious innovation (*bid'ah*),' and Abū Dāwūd related the same narration in the book of the *Sunnah* (*Kitāb al-Sunnah*) from his *Sunan* within the chapter concerning, 'Adherence to the *Sunnah*.' Upon the authority of al-'Irbāḍ Ibn Sāriyah (رضي الله عنه) who said, "The Messenger of Allāh (ﷺ) admonished us one day after the early morning Prayer. The admonition was heartfelt and

[1] Refer to *Naqḍ al-Manṭaq* (p. 42-44) of Ibn Taymiyyah.

eloquent and caused the eyes to shed tears and the hearts to tremble. A man from amongst us said, 'Certainly, it is as if this is a farewell admonition, so with what do you advise us O Messenger of Allāh (ﷺ)?' He replied, 'I advise you to fear Allāh and to hear and obey those in authority over you even if it were an Abyssinnian slave. Indeed, whoever from amongst you lives long will witness much division. And beware of newly invented matters for surely they are misguidance. Whoever from amongst you lives to witness this, then cling to my *Sunnah* and the way of the Rightly Guided Caliphs who will come after me and grab onto it with your molar teeth.'"

According to the wording of Ibn Mājah, [al-'Irbāḍ Ibn Sāriyah] said, "Then the Messenger of Allāh (ﷺ) said, 'I have left you upon clear guidance, its night is like its day. No one strays from it except that they are destroyed. Whoever from amongst you lives long after me will witness great differing. So adhere to what you know of my *Sunnah* and the *Sunnah* of my Rightly-Guided Caliphs, and hold onto it with your molar teeth. And obey the leader even if he is an Abyssinian slave. For the believer is like a camel with a ring in its nose wherever you direct it it will follow.'"[1]

This admonition given by the Messenger of Allāh (ﷺ) is amongst those narrations which comprise of few words but has an immense meaning, and it is comprehensive and precise.

It represents a tremendous foundation from the foundations of this Religion. This is from the angle that people's lives consist of various relationships. It is either his relationship with his Lord, his relationship with his community or his relationship with himself.

This narration clarifies the servant's relationship with Allāh as found in his statement, "I advise you to fear Allāh."

The relationship between the individual and his community is mentioned in his statement, "Hear and obey those in authority even if

[1] This *ḥadīth* is established and its sources have been cited.

it were an Abyssinnian slave. Indeed, whoever from amongst you lives long will witness much differing. Beware of newly invented matters for surely they are misguidance. Whoever from amongst you lives to witness this, then cling to my *Sunnah* and the way of the Rightly-Guided Caliphs who will come after me and grab onto it with your molar teeth."

The relationship that a person has with himself is clarified in the admonition with the mention of *taqwā* (fearing Allāh) and adherence to the *Sunnah.*

This advice also indicates the excellence of following the *Sunnah* of the Messenger of Allāh (ﷺ).

This narration also contains information of what will transpire in the future. What exactly is this event that will occur?

The Messenger of Allāh (ﷺ) informed us that a great amount of differing would occur amongst the Muslims as opposed to his era, "Whoever from amongst you lives long after me will witness great differing."

So what is the path to safety? What is the way to deliverance from this? How can we escape this?

He (ﷺ) said, "Cling to my *Sunnah* and the way of the Rightly-Guided Caliphs who will come after me and grab onto it with your molar teeth."

By adhering to what the Messenger of Allāh (ﷺ) was upon and his Companions will allow you to protect yourself from this blameworthy type of differing. You will also be able to protect yourself from entering into issues of differing and splitting which have been condemned by Islām.

◆◆❖◆◆

The Fifth Characteristic
They Work Towards the Establishment of the Religion through the Seeking of Correct Islāmic Knowledge and its Application

According to them [i.e. the *Salafīs*] knowledge is following the narrations. They collect the *āyāt* [of the *Qur'ān*], *ḥadīth* [of the Messenger of Allāh (ﷺ)] and the narrations of the Companions, and they seek to understand them. They follow the speech of the *Salaf* and do not introduce any new understanding of the texts that departs from the speech of the Companions (رضي الله عنهم).

Ibn Taymiyyah (رحمه الله) said, "The knowledge that is legislated and the rites of worship that are legislated [in this Religion] are taken from the Companions of the Messenger of Allāh (ﷺ). As for what has come from those who succeeded them, then it is inappropriate that this be used as a foundation even though this person maybe excused, rather rewarded for their efforts to extract the correct ruling (*ijtihād*) or their efforts to follow another in a ruling (*taqlīd*). Whoever bases his speech in the various Islāmic sciences - whether they are fundamental issues or secondary issues- upon the Book (the *Qur'ān*), the *Sunnah* and the narrations that have reached us from the earliest generations, then this individual has traversed upon the path of the Prophet. Similarly, the one who bases his intention, his worship, his deeds and his hearing [of knowledge] as it relates to the fundamentals of actions and their subsidiary branches from the affairs of the heart and the actions of the body; whoever bases these things upon true faith, the *Sunnah*, and the guidance of Muḥammad (ﷺ) and his Companions, then he has traversed upon the path of the Prophet. This is the way of the Imāms of guidance.

You find that Imām Aḥmad (d.241H) said after mentioning the foundations of the *Sunnah* (*Uṣūl al-Sunnah*), "It is to adhere to what the Companions of the Messenger of Allāh (ﷺ) were upon." He wrote books of *tafsīr* (Qur'ānic exegesis) which comprised of narrations of the Prophet (ﷺ), his Companions and their students. He wrote books of *ḥadīth* and narrations which comprised of narrations of the Prophet (ﷺ), his Companions and their students. This is what he used to rely upon in both the fundamental issues of knowledge as well as the subsidiary issues; and this is emphasized by a letter that he wrote to the Caliph of his time al-Mutawakkil where he said: 'I do not like speech in any of these matters except that it is found in the Book of Allāh (the *Qur'ān*), the *ḥadīth* of the Messenger of Allāh (ﷺ), or the speech of the Companions or their students. As for the speech that is based upon other than that, then this [type of] speech is censured."

This was also his position concerning asceticism (*zuhd*), matters that soften heart (*raqā'iq*), and the conditions of the heart (*aḥwāl*). In his book entitled *al-Zuhd* (asceticism), he relied upon what has been transmitted from the Prophets - may the peace and blessings of Allāh be upon them - from Ādam to Muḥammad, then he mentioned the narrations of the Companions and their students, without mentioning the statements of those who came after them.

This was also the case when he described how a person should seek knowledge as he advised that [the student] should record, 'What has come from the Prophet (ﷺ), then what has reached us from the Companions and then from their students.' In another narration 'Then you have a choice concerning [the statements of] the students of the Companions.'"[1]

There can be no doubt that knowledge of the statements of the *Salaf*, the Companions and their students, and knowledge of their actions, their consensus and even the matters in which they differed is more valuable than knowing the statements and actions of those who came after them.[2]

If you were to contemplate, you would find that every faction and sect of this great nation of Muḥammad will claim that they adhere to the Book of Allāh (the *Qur'ān*) and the *Sunnah*. However, the criterion which

---

[1] Refer to *Majmū' al-Fatāwā* (10/362-364) of Ibn Taymiyyah.
[2] This has been stated by Ibn Taymiyyah in *Majmū' al-Fatāwā* (13/23-27).

differentiates between these various factions and sects is to carefully examine which of them are upon what the Messenger of Allāh (ﷺ) and his Companions were upon and to then adhere to this. Since this is the saved sect and the group which will be aided, and this is the *Jamāʿah* and the way of the Believers.

Allāh (ﷻ) said,

﴿ وَمَن يُشَاقِقِ ٱلرَّسُولَ مِنۢ بَعْدِ مَا تَبَيَّنَ لَهُ ٱلْهُدَىٰ وَيَتَّبِعْ غَيْرَ سَبِيلِ ٱلْمُؤْمِنِينَ نُوَلِّهِۦ مَا تَوَلَّىٰ وَنُصْلِهِۦ جَهَنَّمَ ۖ وَسَآءَتْ مَصِيرًا ﴿١١٥﴾ ﴾

> **"And whoever opposes the Messenger after guidance has been made clear to him, and follows other than the way of the Believers; We will direct him towards the path which he has chosen, and burn him in Hellfire; and what an evil destination."** [Sūrah al-Nisāʾ 4:115]

Al-Shāfiʿī (رحمه الله) mentioned in the book, *ar-Risālah al-Qadīmah*, after mentioning the Companions and praising them with words of praise that they deserve, "They are far greater than us in every discipline of knowledge and interpretive jurisprudence (*ijtihād*). They are better than us in piety and intellect and any affair of knowledge which requires understanding and extrapolation. Their opinions are more praiseworthy and more deserving of our attention than our own opinions which we formulate ourselves, and Allāh knows best.

Whomever we have encountered from those whom we are pleased with and those whom we have been informed about in our lands relied upon the position of the Companions if they formed a consensus and the position of some of them if they differed, if there was no explicit narration known from the *Sunnah* of the Messenger of Allāh (ﷺ). This is what we state: if they reach a consensus, then we act upon their consensus and promote it. And if one of them held a position that was not opposed by his peers from amongst the companions, then we embrace his position. But if they differed, then we accept the position of some of them without departing from the positions that were held by the Companions."[1]

This methodology is the path that was taken by the Imāms of this Religion and the legislation that was walked upon by those who were guided and traversed upon the Straight Path. This is the knowledge that is both precise and authentic.

All praise belongs to Allāh for the person saying,

الْعِلْمُ قَالَ اللَّهُ قَالَ رَسُولُهُ   قَالَ الصَّحَابَةُ لَيْسَ خُلْفٌ فِيهِ

مَا الْعِلْمُ نَصْبُكَ لِلْخِلَافِ سَفَاهَةً   بَيْنَ النُّصُوصِ وَبَيْنَ رَأْيِ سَفِيهِ

كَلَّا وَلَا نَصْبُ الْخِلَافِ جَهَالَةً   بَيْنَ الرَّسُولِ وَبَيْنَ رَأْيِ فَقِيهِ

كَلَّا وَلَا رَدُّ النُّصُوصِ تَعَمُّدًا   حَذَرًا مِنَ التَّجْسِيمِ وَالتَّشْبِيهِ

"Knowledge is, 'Allāh said, His Messenger said,
the Companions said;' there is no discrepancy therein.

It is not knowledge that you foolishly designate a disagreement,
between the textual evidence and the opinion of a fool.

Nor is it that you ignorantly designate a disagreement,
between the Messenger and the opinion of a jurist.

Nor is it that you deliberately reject the texts,
Out of fear of considering Allāh a body (tajsīm) and resembling Allāh to His creation (tashbīh)."

[1] Refer to *al-Madkhal ilā al-Sunan al-Kubrā* (p. 110).

Al-Awzāʿī (ﷺ) said, "Knowledge is what reaches you from the companions of Muḥammad (ﷺ), and anything else is not considered knowledge."[1]

Al-Zuhrī (ﷺ) used to write down the speech of the students of the Companions while his colleague Ṣāliḥ Ibn al-Kaysān used to oppose him in this practice, and the latter later lived to regret the decision not to record their statements.[2]

Abū Ḥanīfah al-Nuʿmān (ﷺ) proceeded upon this path.

Ibn al-Mubārak (ﷺ) said, "I heard Abū Ḥanīfah (ﷺ) say, 'If something reaches us from the Prophet (ﷺ) then it is more than deserving to be accepted and honoured. If something reaches us from the Companions of the Prophet (ﷺ), then we select one of their positions. If something comes from the students of the Companions, then we may participate with them [to arrive at what is correct].'"[3]

Mālik Ibn Anas al-Aṣbaḥī the Imām of *Dārul-Hijrah* (ﷺ) also proceeded upon this path. When his book, *al-Muwwaṭa'*, was mentioned to him, Mālik said, "It contains *ḥadīth* of the Messenger of Allāh (ﷺ), and the statements of the Companions and their students along with their opinions. I mentioned some of my own opinions which I reached through interpretive jurisprudence (*ijtihād*) and what I have acquired from the people of knowledge in our land. I have not departed whatsoever from their stances."[4]

---

[1] Related by Ibn ʿAbdul-Barr in *Jāmiʿ Bayān al-ʿIlm wa Faḍluhu* (2/29).
[2] Related by al-Khaṭīb al-Baghdādī in *Taqyīd al-ʿIlm* (p. 106-107) and Ibn ʿAbdul-Barr in *Jāmiʿ Bayān al-ʿIlm wa Faḍluhu* (1/76-77), and this has been taken from the comment made by the brother Muḥammad Nāṣir al-ʿAjmī upon *Bayān Faḍl ʿIlm al-Salaf* (p. 69).
[3] Refer to *Akhbār Abū Ḥanīfah* (p. 10) of aṣ-Ṣaymirī, transmitted by Abū Yūsuf from *Abū Ḥanīfah Īqāẓ Himam Ūlī al-Abṣār* (p. 70).
[4] Refer to *Tartīb al-Madārak* (1/193).

This was also the path that was traversed by al-Shāfiʿī (ﷺ). Al-Shāfiʿī (ﷺ) said, "Knowledge consists of levels:

- **The First Level:** The Book of Allāh (the *Qurʾān*) and the *Sunnah* if it has been authentically established in the *Sunnah.*
- **The Second Level:** The scholarly consensus (*ijmāʿ*), when no proof is found in the *Qurʾān* and the *Sunnah.*
- **The Third Level:** When some of the Companions state something and we do not know of any Companion who opposed them.
- **The Fourth Level:** Differing opinions amongst the Companions (ﷺ) of the Prophet (ﷺ).
- **The Fifth Level:** [The correct use of] juristic analogy or inference (*qiyās*) in relation to some of these levels.

Nothing should be sought from other than the *Qurʾān* and the *Sunnah* when the appropriate texts are found. For indeed knowledge is sought from the top."[1]

This is also the methodology of Aḥmad Ibn Muḥammad Ibn Ḥanbal (ﷺ). Aḥmad Ibn Muḥammad Ibn Ḥanbal said, "If there is a *ḥadīth* concerning a specific issue that was reported from the Prophet (ﷺ), then we do not accept a statement from any of the Companions or those who came after them in opposition to it.

If the Companions of the Messenger of Allāh (ﷺ) held different positions about an issue then we choose from their positions. We do not depart from their positions and [accept the stance] of others.

If there is no statement from the Prophet (ﷺ) or his Companions in an issue, then we choose from the positions of the students of the Companions..."[2]

---

[1] Refer to *al-Madkhal ilā al-Sunan al-Kubrā* (p. 110).
[2] Refer to *al-Musawwadah* (p. 276).

Muḥammad Ibn al-Ḥasan said, "Whoever is a Scholar concerning the Book of Allāh (the *Qur'ān*), the *Sunnah*, the statements of the Companions of the Messenger of Allāh (ﷺ) and what is considered sound by the Muslim jurists, then [this individual has] extensive insight that allows him to conduct interpretive jurisprudence (*ijtihād*) that will shape his opinion in matters which are pertinent to him. This individual can judge in accordance with this and implement his judgment in his Prayer, fasting, *Ḥajj* and everything that he has been commanded with and forbidden from. So if he performs interpretive jurisprudence (*ijtihād*), examines the situation and compares it (*qiyās*) to a similar situation, then he did not fall short with this effort even if he did not reach the correct position."[1]

Muḥammad Ibn al-Ḥasan also said, "Knowledge is of four types:

- What can be clearly found in the Book of Allāh (the *Qur'ān*), and whatever is similar to this. And what is found in the *Sunnah* of the Messenger of Allāh (ﷺ), and whatever is similar to this.
- Whatever the Companions unanimously agreed upon, and whatever is similar to this.
- Likewise those issues which the Companions differed concerning. No one should depart from the positions of the Companions. If a person chooses from the opinions of the Companions, then this is knowledge which can be used for juristic analogy, and whatever may resemble this.
- Whatever is deemed to be correct by the majority of Muslim jurists, and whatever is similar to this.

Knowledge does not consist of any classification other than these four."[2]

I say: Their words are the same, may Allāh have mercy upon them, and they all have agreed upon this methodology. So whoever departs from

[1] Related by Ibn 'Abdul-Barr in *Jāmi' Bayān al-'Ilm wa Faḍluhu* (2 /61).
[2] Related by Ibn 'Abdul-Barr in *Jāmi' Bayān al-'Ilm wa Faḍluhu* (2/26).

it has departed from the path of the Believers. And Allāh is the One who grants success.

Ibn Taymiyyah (؈) said, "Whoever explains the *Qur'ān* or *ḥadīth* and interprets it in a way other than that which was known to the Companions and their students is a fabricator of a lie against Allāh, a distorter of the *āyāt* of Allāh and one who misinterprets words from their true context. This action opens the door to infidelity (*zandaqah*) and heresy (*ilḥād*). The falsehood of such a practice is well known by necessity in the Religion of Islām."[1]

It is impermissible for anyone to interpret a verse of the *Qur'ān* or *ḥadīth* with a meaning that directly contradicts and opposes the meaning [found in the] explanation given by the Companions of the Messenger (؈).

Ibn Rajab (؈) said, "In our time [And I say (Shaykh Bazmool) that in our time it is even more applicable] it is necessary to record the speech of the Imāms of the *Salaf* whose example should be followed all the way up until the time of al-Shāfiʿī, Aḥmad, Isḥāq (d.238H), and Abū ʿUbayd (d.224H). This is so that an individual can be cautious regarding what occurred after them. For indeed, many things happened after them. People began to ascribe themselves to the *Sunnah* and *ḥadīth* from the literalists (*Ẓāhiriyyah*) and those who resemble them, yet they are of the worst in terms of their opposition to it because of their deviation from the Imāms, them establishing their own understanding and them taking something that none of the Imāms before them took.[2]"

Due to this principle, and this is referring to understanding the Glorious *Qur'ān* and the Prophetic *Sunnah* in light of the understanding of the Companions (؈), you see that the people of the *Sunnah* and the *Jamāʿah*, the people of *ḥadīth* do not delve into issues like explaining the Glorious *Qur'ān* and clarifying the meanings of *ḥadīth* by solely relying upon the Arabic language, opinion, and intellect. Contrary to that, they

---

[1] Refer to *Majmūʿ Fatāwā* (13/ 243) of Ibn Taymiyyah.
[2] Refer to *Bayān Faḍl ʿIlm as-Salaf* (p. 69).

look at and study the narrations and they gather whatever is found in the works of the *Salaf*. They base their jurisprudence (*fiqh*) and their interpretive jurisprudence (*ijtihād*) upon this as opposed to the people of desires and innovation (*bidʿah*).

Ibn Taymiyyah (ﷺ) said, "The *Murjiʾah* deviated in this principle [referring to the issue of faith (*īmān*)] from the clarity of the Book (the *Qurʾān*), the *Sunnah* and the statements of the Companions and their students who followed them in goodness. They chose to rely upon their own opinion and what they interpreted through their own understanding of the Arabic language. This is the way of the people of innovation (*bidʿah*). That is why Imām Aḥmad used to say, "The main reason that people make mistakes is misinterpretation and analogy (*qiyās*)."

This is why we find the *Muʿtazilah*, the *Murjiʾah*, the *Rāfiḍah* and the rest of the people of innovation (*bidʿah*) explaining the *Qurʾān* according to their own opinion, intellects and whatever they can derive from the Arabic language. You will find that they do not rely upon the *ḥadīth* of the Prophet (ﷺ) or the narrations of the Companions and their students or the Imāms of the Muslims. They do not rely upon the *Sunnah* or the consensus of the *Salaf* and their narrations but they restrict themselves solely to the intellect and the Arabic language.

We find that they do not rely upon the books of *tafsīr* (Qurʾānic exegesis) that comprise of narrations, the books of *ḥadīth* and the books that contain the narrations of the *Salaf*. Instead, they only rely upon books of Arabic literature and books of rhetoric and theory that were compiled by their figureheads. This is also the way of the heretics (*malāḥidah*). They too restrict themselves to the books of philosophy, literature and Arabic language but as for the books that focus on the *Qurʾān*, *ḥadīth* and narrations then they do not even look in their direction.

These groups turn their backs on the texts of the Prophets since according to them these texts do not convey certain knowledge [i.e. this knowledge is speculative]. So they interpret the *Qurʾān* according to their opinions and their own understanding with no narrations from the Prophet (ﷺ) or his Companions. We have already mentioned the speech of Imām Aḥmad and other than him in refutation of this practice and his declaration that this is from the ways of the people of innovation (*bidʿah*)."[1]

I say: Imām Aḥmad (رحمه الله) said, "Beware of speaking in an issue that you have not been preceded in by an Imām."[2]

The abandonment of the *ḥadīth* and *Salafī* narrations and totally depending upon the books of language and rhetoric to understand the *Qurʾān* and *ḥadīth* is a path taken in this era by the orientalists. If their research requires them to search for some narrations, they cite *al-Jāḥiẓ*, the book, *al-Aghānī*, or *al-ʿAqd al-Farīd*. If they feel uncomfortable to cite textual evidence, then they say, 'This is what is necessitated by the intellect.'

So the Muslim who follows the way of the Prophet (ﷺ) and his Companions restricts his learning and understanding of the Glorious Qurʾān and Prophetic *Sunnah* to the understanding of the Companions (رضي الله عنهم) and he does not look to other than them. However, if a particular issue seems to require interpretive jurisprudence (*ijtihād*) or further examination, he first looks to determine whether or not he has any predecessor [in the conclusion he has reached]. If not then he abandons this position since all good comes from following the *Salaf* and all evil comes from following the latter generations [who deviated from the path of the *Salaf*].

It is incumbent that you cling to that which is ancient [i.e. the way of *Salaf*].

---

[1] Refer to *Īmān* (p. 114).

[2] Cited in *Majmūʿ al-Fatāwā* (21/291); and it has been presented along with its chain by Ibn al-Jawzī in the book *Manāqib al-Imām Aḥmad Ibn Ḥanbal* (p. 178).

Ibn Ḥajr (ﷺ) said, 'Al-Awzā'ī said, 'Knowledge is what has come to us from the Companions of the Messenger of Allāh (ﷺ), and whatever did not come from them is not considered knowledge."

And Abū 'Ubayd and Ya'qūb Ibn Shaybah collected by way of Ibn Mas'ūd that he said, 'The people will continue to remain in a state of good, as long as they take their knowledge from the Companions of Muḥammad (ﷺ) and their elders. If they take their knowledge from the lesser ones amongst them and split because of their desires they will be destroyed.' Abū 'Ubaydah said, 'This means that everything that has come from the Companions and their senior students who followed them in goodness is the knowledge which has been inherited. Whatever has been introduced [into the religion] after them is blameworthy. The *Salaf* used to differentiate between knowledge and opinion. They stated that the *Sunnah* is knowledge and whatever opposes it is opinion.'

It has been narrated from Aḥmad that knowledge is to be taken from the Prophet (ﷺ), then from the Companions and if there is nothing from them then you have a choice concerning [the statements of] the students of the Companions.'

It has also been narrated that [he said], 'Whatever is reported from the Rightly Guided Caliphs is from the *Sunnah*, and if someone was to say that whatever is reported from any of the Companions is a *Sunnah* then I would not reject it.'

It has been reported that Ibn al-Mubārak (ﷺ) said, 'The narration is that which should be relied upon, and only use opinion in situations where it will aid in explaining the narration.'

In summary, if the opinion is based upon the textual evidence of the *Qur'ān* and the *Sunnah* it is praiseworthy. However, if it is used independently without knowledge [of the *Qur'ān* and the *Sunnah*] then it is blameworthy."[1]

---

[1] Refer to *Fatḥ al-Bārī* (13/291). Many of the narrations cited in this passage have already been referenced –and all praise and favour is due to Allāh.

This characteristic necessitates the following:

1. That the *Salafīs* do not speak about matters of the Religion with their opinions or intellects. ʿAlī (☺) said, "If the Religion was according to opinion, then the bottom of the *khuf* (leather socks) would be more deserving to be wiped as opposed to the top. But indeed, I saw the Messenger of Allāh (☺) wipe the top of his *khufs*." In another wording of this narration he said, "I believed that the bottom of the leather socks was the most deserving part to be washed, until I saw the Messenger of Allāh (☺) wipe over the top of his *khufs*." In another wording he said, 'If the Religion was based upon the intellect then the bottom of the feet would be more deserving to be wiped than the top. Verily, I saw the Messenger of Allāh (☺) wipe over the top of his *khufs*." Collected by Abū Dāwūd.[1]

Abū ʿAbdullāh Muḥammad Ibn Ibrāhīm al-Būshanjī (☺) said, "It is obligatory upon all of the people of knowledge and the people of Islām to be intent upon following [i.e. the Book and the *Sunnah*]. They should make the principles that were revealed in the *Qurʾān* and found in the *Sunnah* of the Messenger (☺) the focus of their intellects. They should not make their intellects the focus and basis from which they derive principles."[2]

Abū al-Muẓaffar al-Samʿānī (☺) said, "As for the people of the truth, then they have placed the Book (the *Qurʾān*) and the *Sunnah* in front of them and sought the Religion from them. They examined whatever thoughts and intellectual arguments they developed in light of the Book (the *Qurʾān*) and the *Sunnah*. If they find that it is consistent with what has been revealed, then they thank Allāh (☺) since He directed them to

---

[1] This *ḥadīth* is authentic. Related by Abū Dāwūd (no. 162). Shaykh al-Albānī has authenticated this narration in *Ṣaḥīḥ Sunan Abī Dāwud* (1/33).
[2] Refer to *Dhamm al-Kalām* by al-Harawī, by way of the book *Ṣawn al-Manṭaq wa al-Kalām* (p. 69).

it and granted them success. On the other hand, if they find that it opposes the [Book and *Sunnah*], then they abandon this and turn sincerely to the Book (the *Qur'ān*) and the *Sunnah* and they assign any blame or doubt to themselves. Indeed, the Book (the *Qur'ān*) and the *Sunnah* can only guide people to the truth but the people's opinions can sometimes conform to the truth and sometimes be absolutely wrong."[1]

He (رحمه الله) also said, "As for the people of the *Sunnah*, may Allāh preserve them, then they cling to whatever is found in the Book (the *Qur'ān*) and the *Sunnah*, and they establish this with clear evidences and authentic proof according to the Islāmic legislation and according to what has been revealed. They do not speak concerning Allāh's (سبحانه وتعالى) Attributes or any other affair of the Religion based upon their opinions. This was the way that they found their predecessors (*Salaf*) and their Imāms upon.

Allāh (سبحانه وتعالى) said,

﴿ يَٰٓأَيُّهَا ٱلنَّبِيُّ إِنَّآ أَرْسَلْنَٰكَ شَٰهِدًا وَمُبَشِّرًا وَنَذِيرًا ﴿٤٥﴾ وَدَاعِيًا إِلَى
ٱللَّهِ بِإِذْنِهِۦ وَسِرَاجًا مُّنِيرًا ﴿٤٦﴾ ﴾

"O Prophet! Indeed, We have sent you as a witness, a bearer of glad tidings, a warner, and one who invites to Allāh by His permission, and as an illuminating lamp."
[Sūrah al-Aḥzāb 33:45-46]

[1] Refer to *al-Intiṣār li Ahl al-Ḥadīth* of Abū al-Muẓaffar al-Samʿānī, by way of the book *Ṣawn al-Manṭaq wa al-Kalām* (p. 166-167).

And He also said,

﴿ ۞ يَٰٓأَيُّهَا ٱلرَّسُولُ بَلِّغۡ مَآ أُنزِلَ إِلَيۡكَ مِن رَّبِّكَۖ وَإِن لَّمۡ تَفۡعَلۡ فَمَا بَلَّغۡتَ رِسَالَتَهُۥۚ ﴾

"O Messenger, convey what has been revealed to you from your Lord, and if you do not, then you have not transmited His message." [Sūrah al-Mā'idah 5:67]

The Prophet (ﷺ) said in his farewell sermon [*khuṭbah*], and in many other situations in the presence of his Companions (رضي الله عنهم), "Have I not conveyed [the message]?"[1] Islāmic monotheism (*Tawḥīd*) is amongst those affairs which were revealed to him and which he was commanded to convey and explain. The Prophet (ﷺ) did not neglect any matter of the Religion, its fundamentals, principles, legislation and tenets, except that he clarified and conveyed it perfectly and completely. He did not delay clarifying these things until after the need had passed. This is because had he done this, he would have burdened his Companions with something beyond their capacity."[2]

He (رحمه الله) also said, "We have been commanded to follow and adhere to the narrations of the Prophet (ﷺ), and to cling to what he has legislated for us in the Religion and the *Sunnah*. It is not possible for us to achieve this except through the text

[1] This statement has been authentically transmitted from the Messenger of Allāh (ﷺ) on various occassions as the Imām indicated. This statement is found in the story of Ibn al-Lutbiyyah from the narration of Abū Humayd as-Sā'idī (رضي الله عنه) which is in al-Bukhārī (no. 7197), the *khuṭbah* of *Kusūf* from the narrations of 'Ā'ishah (رضي الله عنها) in Muslim (no. 901), and the *khuṭbah* from the day of sacrifice from the narration of Abū Bakrah in al-Bukhārī (no. 1741) and in Muslim (no. 1679).

[2] Refer to *al-Intiṣār li Ahl al-Ḥadīth* of Abū al-Muẓaffar al-Sam'ānī, by way of the book *Ṣawn al-Manṭaq wa al-Kalām* (p. 175). Compare this to the speech of al-Khaṭṭābī in his treatise, *al-Ghunyah 'an al-Kalām*, by way of the book *Ṣawn al-Manṭaq wa al-Kalām* (p. 95-96).

and *ḥadīth*, following the narrations that the trustworthy and reliable people of this nation have conveyed from the Messenger of Allāh (ﷺ), his Companions and those who came after them. So now we will explain the statement of the people of the *Sunnah*: Verily, the path of the Religion involves submitting to the texts [of the Book and *Sunnah*] and the narrations. As for the [approach of just relying upon] the intellect, referring to it and basing what has been narrated upon it, then this is blameworthy in the Religion and prohibited. We will discuss the place of the intellect in the Religion and the extent that the Religion has commanded us to utilize it and the limits it has set which are impermissible to exceed..."[1]

His student, the guardian of the *Sunnah* [Abūl-Qāsim Ismāʿīl ibn Muḥammad] al-Aṣbahānī (رحمه الله) said, "This is because the affairs of the religion have been clarified for the people so all we have to do is follow since the Religion has come solely from Allāh and is not to be subjected to the intellects of men and their opinions. The Messenger of Allāh (ﷺ) has clarified the *Sunnah* to his nation and explained it to his Companions. So whoever opposes the Companions of the Messenger of Allāh (ﷺ) in any affair from the Religion has certainly gone astray."[2]

He said, "We do not oppose the *Sunnah* of the Messenger of Allāh (ﷺ) with our logic. This is because the Religion itself [is comprehended by using] the intellect [to understand the texts] because the intellect leads to the acceptance of the *Sunnah*, and as for what leads a person to abandonment of the *Sunnah* then this is ignorance and not intelligence."[3]

---

[1] Refer to *al-Intiṣār li Ahl al-Ḥadīth* of Abū al-Muẓaffar al-Samʿānī, by way of the book *Ṣawn al-Manṭaq wa al-Kalām* (p. 148).
[2] Refer to *al-Ḥujjah fī Bayān al-Maḥajjah* (2/440).
[3] Refer to *al-Ḥujjah fī Bayān al-Maḥajjah* (2/509).

2. They honour the people of knowledge, respect them and fulfil their rights without neglecting any of them. Abū al-Dardā' (رضي الله عنه) said, "I heard the Messenger of Allāh (ﷺ) saying, 'Whoever travels a path seeking knowledge, Allāh will place him on a path leading to Paradise. The angels lower their wings for the student of knowledge, pleased with what he is doing. The inhabitants of the heavens and earth seek forgiveness for the student of knowledge, even the fish in the water. The superiority of the Scholar over the devout worshipper is like the superiority of the full moon over the the rest of the stars. The Scholars are the heirs of the Prophets. The Prophets leave no money [*dinār* or *dirham*] as an inheritance, rather they leave knowledge. Whoever seizes it takes an abundant portion.'"[1]

   Abū Ḥātim Ibn Ḥibbān (رحمه الله) said, "In this narration is a clear indication that the Scholars who possess the virtue that we have mentioned teach the people the knowledge of the Prophet (ﷺ) as opposed to other types of knowledge. Do you not notice that he said that the Scholars are the heirs of the Prophets? And the Prophets do not leave behind anything but knowledge. The knowledge of our Prophet (ﷺ) is his *Sunnah*. Whoever lacks this knowledge of the *Sunnah* cannot be from the inheritors of the Prophets."[2]

   Allāh (سبحانه وتعالى) said,

﴿ وَإِذَا جَآءَهُمۡ أَمۡرٞ مِّنَ ٱلۡأَمۡنِ أَوِ ٱلۡخَوۡفِ أَذَاعُواْ بِهِۦۖ وَلَوۡ رَدُّوهُ إِلَى
ٱلرَّسُولِ وَإِلَىٰٓ أُوْلِي ٱلۡأَمۡرِ مِنۡهُمۡ لَعَلِمَهُ ٱلَّذِينَ يَسۡتَنۢبِطُونَهُۥ مِنۡهُمۡۗ وَلَوۡلَا
فَضۡلُ ٱللَّهِ عَلَيۡكُمۡ وَرَحۡمَتُهُۥ لَٱتَّبَعۡتُمُ ٱلشَّيۡطَٰنَ إِلَّا قَلِيلٗا ٨٣ ﴾

---

[1] This *ḥadīth* is *Ḥasan* (sound).The sources for this narration has been cited earlier.
[2] Refer to *al-Iḥsān bi Taqrīb Ṣaḥīḥ Ibn Ḥibbān* (1/295, no. 88).

"When there comes to them some matter concerning [public] safety or fear, [which] they spread; if only they had referred it back to the Messenger or to those in authority among them, then the ones who can derive the proper conclusions would have known about it. And if it were not for the favor of Allāh upon you and His mercy, you would have all certainly followed *Shayṭān* except for very few." [Sūrah al-Nisā' 4:83]

In this verse is an instruction to refer back to the people of knowledge in the occurrence of a severe calamity or affliction, and that rulings related to this event should be sought from them; and judgements should not be sought from others beside them nor should anyone precede them in addressing these issues. Also this verse shows that referring to the people of opinion involves rejection of the command of Allāh (ﷻ) to return these affairs to the Scholars who are able to derive the proper rulings. This is because the people of opinion are not people who can derive the proper verdicts. **So no one should precede them in producing public statements or public declarations relating to current events.** Rather, they should be referred to as this is their right.

'Abd al-Raḥmān Ibn Nāṣir as-Sa'dī (رحمه الله) said in his explanation of this noble *āyah*, "This is a piece of disciplinary admonition from Allāh to His servants concerning their inappropriate behavior. It is proper when news reaches them of important issues or things that are of a general benefit [to the Muslims]- such as the issues connected to public welfare and the safety of the Believers or fear of a calamity befalling them- that they should first verify such news and not be hasty to spread it. Instead, they should refer these issues back to the Messenger (ﷺ) and those in authority from amongst them, those who are people of sound opinion, knowledge, sincere advice, intellect and composure, those who understand the affairs and are able to recognize the associated benefits and harms.

If they believe that it is beneficial to broadcast these affairs and that it will increase the spirit of the Believers, bring them tranquility and protect them from their enemies then they [spread this news].

On the other hand, if they believe that there is no benefit in this or that there is some benefit but the harms outweigh them, then they do not broadcast this news.

This is why Allāh said, "**The ones who can derive the proper conclusions would have known about it.**"

This means that they would extract the ruling through the use of their abilities, sound opinions and correct knowledge. In this is an evidence for the ethical principle which states that if the need arises to research a particular situation, then it is essential that it be left to those best qualified for it, and nobody should precede them in this.

This is the most correct and safest approach which minimizes the potential for error.

In this [*āyah*] there is also the prohibition of being hasty and rushing to spread news upon hearing it, and a command to reflect before speaking and to examine the issue as to whether there is any benefit in [speaking] which would cause a person to continue to utter it or harm which would cause him to refrain.

Then Allāh says, "**And if it were not for the favor of Allāh upon you and His mercy.**"

This is referring to the success that He has granted you, the education that He has provided you with and how He taught you things that you did not know.

"**You would have all certainly followed Shayṭān except for very few.**"

This is because mankind according to his very nature is oppressive and ignorant and his soul only incites him towards evil. But if he returns to his Lord, holds firmly to him and struggles in doing this, then Allāh will make things easy for him and guide him towards everything good and protect him from the accursed *Shayṭān*."[1]

The abandonment of returning to the scholars involves blatant disregard of their rights, and many evils result from this:

From them is that this will result in disgrace and humiliation afflicting this nation. This is highlighted in the narration of Ibn ʿUmar (ﷺ) who said, 'I heard the Messenger of Allāh (ﷺ) say, 'When you begin to deal with usury, take hold of the tails of cows, become pleased with agriculture and abandon *Jihād*, then Allāh will place upon you a humiliation and He will not lift it until you return to your Religion."[2]

There is no way for the people to return back to the Religion except by way of the Scholars. If the people were to neglect the rights of the Scholars, and started not to return to them and in fact neglected them, and took ignorant figureheads and idealogues, how could they possibly return to the Religion?

---

[1] Refer to *Taysīr al-Karīm al-Raḥmān*, from edition that is printed in the margin of the Glorious *Qurʾān* (p. 190). Also compare this with what was written in *Maḥāsin al-Taʾwīl* by al-Qāsimī (5/324-326).

[2] Related by Aḥmad in *al-Musnad* (*al-Risālah*, 8/440, no. 4725, 9/51, no. 5007, 9/395, 5562); and by Abū Dāwūd (no. 3462), Abū Yaʿlā in his *Musnad* (10/29, no. 5659) and al-Bayhaqī in *al-Sunan al-Kubrā* (5/316). Those who checked the *Musnad* declared this narration to be weak however the checker of the *Musnad* of Abū Yaʿlā indicated that it is sound (*ḥasan*). Shaykh al-Albānī has authenticated this narration due to its multiple chains of narration and has included it in his *Silsilah al-Aḥādīth al-Ṣaḥīḥah* (no. 11). This *ḥadīth* has a supporting narration that has been narrated upon Ibn Masʿūd, which is *marfūʿ* (*ḥadīth* of the Prophet), "Do not take to the estate, so much so that you begin to desire the life of this world." This *ḥadīth* has been collected by Aḥmad in *al-Musnad* (*al-Risālah,* 6 /54, no. 3579), al-Tirmidhī and al-Ḥākim. It was included by Shaykh al-Albānī in his *Silsilah al-Aḥādīth al-Ṣaḥīḥah* (no. 13).

The Religion is as it was described in the narration of Jibrīl wherein Islām, *īmān*, *iḥsān* and the signs of the Day of Judgment were mentioned. It is mentioned at the end of this narration [that ʿUmar said], "Then he left (meaning the questioner who came forth with a strange appearance). I remained for some time. Then he (ﷺ) said to me, "O ʿUmar, do you know who the questioner was?" I replied, Allāh and His Messenger know best. He said, "That was Jibrīl who came to you to teach you your Religion."[1]

If the Scholars are eliminated and the people take for themselves ignorant figureheads and ideologues, then who will guide the people back to their Religion? How could they ever hope to remove the condition of disgrace and humiliation without the Scholars?

From them is that this is a departure from the path of the Believers which is a conduct that carries the threat of the Hellfire for those who adopt it.

And Allāh (سبحانه وتعالى) said,

﴿ وَمَن يُشَاقِقِ ٱلرَّسُولَ مِنۢ بَعۡدِ مَا تَبَيَّنَ لَهُ ٱلۡهُدَىٰ وَيَتَّبِعۡ غَيۡرَ سَبِيلِ
ٱلۡمُؤۡمِنِينَ نُوَلِّهِۦ مَا تَوَلَّىٰ وَنُصۡلِهِۦ جَهَنَّمَۖ وَسَآءَتۡ مَصِيرًا ١١٥ ﴾

"And whoever opposes the Messenger after guidance has been made clear to him, and follows other than the way of the Believers; We will direct him towards the path which he has chosen, and burn him in Hell - and what an evil destination." [Sūrah al-Nisāʾ 4:115]

Amongst the harms that result from neglecting the rights of the Scholars is contradicting the command of the Messenger of

---

[1] Related by Muslim in (no. 8), upon the authority of ʿUmar Ibn al-Khaṭṭāb (رضي الله عنه).

Allāh (ﷻ) to respect the Scholars, preserve their rights and avoid harming them.

And Allāh (ﷻ) said,

﴿ فَلْيَحْذَرِ ٱلَّذِينَ يُخَالِفُونَ عَنْ أَمْرِهِۦٓ أَن تُصِيبَهُمْ فِتْنَةٌ أَوْ يُصِيبَهُمْ عَذَابٌ أَلِيمٌ ﴾

"So let those who oppose his order [beware] **lest an affliction befall them or a severe punishment."**
[Sūrah al-Nūr 24:63]

Amongst the harms of neglecting the rights of the Scholars is agreeing with the people of innovation (*bidʿah*) and desires, and resembling them. This is because it is from the way of the people of innovation (*bidʿah*) and desires to belittle the Scholars. Examine, if you will, the various sects and groups that have opposed the guidance of the Messenger (ﷺ) and that which the companions were upon, and you will most certainly find this trait. As for the *Shīʿah* then their affair is well-known.[1] The Kharijites (*Khawārij*), then their true state has been documented and mentioned[2]. The *Muʿtazilah*, then their situation is notorious.[3] The *Ṣūfīs* and their attacks upon the

---

[1] They have rejected the Companions and condemned them all except for the people of the Prophetic household and whoever else they claim supported them.
[2] They did not restrict themselves to attacking and belittling the Companions; they actually fought against them.
[3] They label the people of the *Sunnah* as: *al-Ḥashwiyyah* and say that they are the carriers of books and that they do not possess any knowledge. In the book, al-*Ḍuʿafāʾ* (3/285), of al-ʿUqaylī, there occurs: Ismāʿīl Ibn ʿUlayyah reported from al-Yasʿ Abū Saʿdah that he said, "Wāṣil was speaking one day and ʿAmr ibn ʿUbayd said: Listen! The speech of al-Ḥasan, Ibn Sīrīn, al-Nakhaʿī, and al-Shaʿbī is nothing more than a discarded menstrual rag." Wāṣil ibn ʿAṭāʾ andʿAmr ibn ʿUbayd are the heads of the *Muʿtazilah*.

Scholars of the Book (the *Qur'ān*) and the *Sunnah* have also been noticed.[1]

You will not find a sect, group or faction that deviates from the straight path and exits from the way of the Believers except that they speak ill of the scholars, ridicule and attack them, neglect their rights and take the ignorant ones as figureheads and idealogues.

Al-Shāṭibī (رحمه الله) said, "It was narrated that one of the leaders of the people of innovation (*bid'ah*) wanted to give precedence to *al-Kalām* [or what is generally considered rhetoric and philosophical conjecture] over *fiqh* (Islāmic jurisprudence). So this individual used to say, 'The knowledge of al-Shāfi'ī and Abū Ḥanīfah does not extend beyond the pants of the women (referring to the rulings of menstruation and postnatal bleeding).' This is the speech of these deviants, may Allāh fight them."[2]

Also from the harms of neglecting the rights of the Scholars is that this results in the people falling into misguidance and them departing from the path of guidance and correctness. This is because the people will take the ignorant as leaders instead of the Scholars. They will consult them and they will give religious rulings which are not based upon knowledge so they will go astray. Thus, from the harms of this is that people will fall into misguidance.

This has been mentioned in the narration which was transmitted upon the authority of 'Amr Ibn al-'Āṣ (رضي الله عنه) who said, 'I heard the Messenger of Allāh (ﷺ) say 'Allāh does not seize the knowledge by snatching it from the people. But rather He seizes the knowledge by the deaths of the Scholars. So if He

---

[1] They sarcastically say about the people of the *Sunnah*: Your knowledge comes from the dead who have narrated from the dead while our knowledge comes from the All Living who will never die. My heart tells me about my Lord.

[2] Refer to *al-I'tiṣām* (2/239) of al-Shāṭibī.

> does not leave a single Scholar the people will take the ignorant as their leaders. These individuals will be questioned and they will issue rulings without knowledge and as a result they go astray and lead others astray."[1]

The part of this *ḥadīth* that is relative here is, "These individuals will be questioned and they will issue rulings without knowledge and as a result they go astray and lead others astray." Look how he judged that they are misguided and that they will lead others astray.

---

[1] Related by al-Bukhārī (no. 100) and Muslim (no. 2673).

The Third Objective
The Way to Achieve Rectification According To the People of the *Sunnah* and the *Jamāʿah*

Change is something that Allāh has decreed for His creation. It has come in the *ḥadīth* which was narrated by al-ʿIrbāḍ Ibn Sāriyah (ﷺ) who said, "The Messenger of Allāh (ﷺ) admonished us one day after the early morning Prayer. The admonition was heartfelt and eloquent and caused the eyes to shed tears and the hearts to tremble. A man from amongst us said, 'Certainly, it is as if this is a farewell admonition, so with what do you advise us, O Messenger of Allāh (ﷺ)?' He replied, 'I advise you to fear Allāh and to hear and obey those in authority over you even if it were an Abyssinnian slave. **Indeed, whoever from amongst you lives long will witness much division.** And beware of newly invented matters for surely they are misguidance. Whoever from amongst you lives to witness this, then cling to my *Sunnah* and the way of the Rightly Guided *Khulafāʾ* [caliphs] who will come after me and grab onto it with your molar teeth.'"

According to the wording of Ibn Mājah, [al-ʿIrbāḍ ibn Sāriyah] said, 'Then the Messenger of Allāh (ﷺ) said, 'I have left you upon clear guidance, its night is like its day. No one strays from it except that they are destroyed. **Whoever from amongst you lives long after me will witness great differing.** So adhere to what you know of my Sunnah and the *Sunnah* of my Rightly Guided Successors (caliphs), and hold onto it with your molar teeth. And obey the leader even if he is an Abyssinian slave. Verily the Believer is like a camel with a ring in its nose wherever you direct it, it will follow."[1]

The part of this narration which is relative here is his statement, "Whoever from amongst you lives long after me will witness great differing." This means that change will occur after the death of the Messenger (ﷺ).

[1] This *ḥadīth* is established and the sources have been cited.

Another proof which substantiates what I have stated is what has been reported by Sālim who said, "I heard Umm al-Dardā' say, 'Abū ad-Dardā' came to me and he was angry.' So I said to him, 'What has upset you?' He said, 'By Allāh, I do not recognize anything from the nation of Muḥammad (ﷺ) except that they pray in congregation together.'"[1]

Al-Ḥāfiẓ Ibn Hajr (d.852H) said, "His statement, 'That they pray in congregation' means that they would do this together. The object (*maf'ūl*) was omitted here and it is understood to be (*taqdīr*) 'Prayer or Prayers'. [Therefore, the meaning would be: That they pray **the Prayers** in congregation]. The intent of Abū al-Dardā' was that there was a deficiency and change that crept into the actions of those individuals that he was referring to except for their gathering to perform the Prayer in congregation. This matter is relative [to his time]. This is because the condition of the people during the time of prophethood was far more complete than the state of the people after this period. Then the condition of the people during the time of the two Shaykhs [Abū Bakr and 'Umar (رضي الله عنهما)] was far more complete than the state of the people after this period. It is as if Abū al-Dardā' made this statement towards the latter portion of his life, and this was towards the end of the Caliphate of 'Uthmān (رضي الله عنه). If this praiseworthy generation was described by Abū al-Dardā' in this fashion, then what could be said about the generations that followed all the way up until our time?"[2]

Thus, change has already occurred in this nation. That is why the Messenger of Allāh (ﷺ) informed us concerning the revival of the Religion. Abū Hurayrah (رضي الله عنه) narrated that the Messenger of Allāh (ﷺ) said, "Indeed, Allāh sends to this nation at the head of every one hundred years those who will revive its Religion."[3]

The meaning of revival, as explained in *'Awn al-Ma'būd,* is to revive acting upon those things found in the Book (the *Qur'ān*) and the *Sunnah* that had been effaced, to command in accordance to them and to curb

---

[1] Related by al-Bukhārī (no. 650).
[2] Refer to *Fatḥ al-Bārī* (2/138) of Ibn Hajr and *Ighāthah al-Lahafān* (1/207) of Ibn al-Qayyim.
[3] Related by Abū Dāwūd (no. 4291).

and subdue innovations (*bid'ah*) and newly invented matters in the Religion.

So there has been change and differences have occurred in comparison to the original state of affairs [of this nation]. The cure for this is to return to the Religion. This is the meaning of rectification.

The correct way to achieve rectification according to those who follow the pious predecessors (*al-Salaf al-Ṣāliḥ*), the People of the *Sunnah* and the *Jamā'ah* is contained within five key guidelines, and they are:

The First Measure
The Beginning and Foundation of this Rectification is the Worship of Allāh and Singling Him Out with Islāmic Monotheism (*Tawḥīd*)

This was the call of all of the Prophets, since every Prophet was sent by Allāh to his people with this message.

And Allāh (ﷻ) said,

﴿ وَلَقَدْ بَعَثْنَا فِي كُلِّ أُمَّةٍ رَّسُولًا أَنِ ٱعْبُدُوا۟ ٱللَّهَ وَٱجْتَنِبُوا۟
ٱلطَّٰغُوتَ ۖ فَمِنْهُم مَّنْ هَدَى ٱللَّهُ وَمِنْهُم مَّنْ حَقَّتْ عَلَيْهِ
ٱلضَّلَٰلَةُ ۚ فَسِيرُوا۟ فِي ٱلْأَرْضِ فَٱنظُرُوا۟ كَيْفَ كَانَ عَٰقِبَةُ
ٱلْمُكَذِّبِينَ ﴿٣٦﴾ ﴾

"And certainly We have sent to every nation a Messenger [commanding them to] **worship Allāh alone and avoid the *ṭāghūt*. From among them were those whom Allāh guided, and among them were those for whom misguidance was** [deservedly] **decreed. So travel throughout the earth and consider the plight of those who denied** [the truth]**."** [Sūrah al-Naḥl 16:36]

And concerning Noah [Nūḥ] (عليه السلام), Allāh (ﷻ) said,

﴿ لَقَدْ أَرْسَلْنَا نُوحًا إِلَىٰ قَوْمِهِۦ فَقَالَ يَٰقَوْمِ ٱعْبُدُوا۟ ٱللَّهَ مَا لَكُم
مِّنْ إِلَٰهٍ غَيْرُهُۥٓ إِنِّيٓ أَخَافُ عَلَيْكُمْ عَذَابَ يَوْمٍ عَظِيمٍ ﴿٥٩﴾ ﴾

"Indeed, We have sent Noah (Nūḥ) to his people, and he said: O my people, worship Allāh; you have no deity other than Him. Certainly, I fear for you the punishment of an overwhelming Day."
[Sūrah al-Aʿrāf 7:59]

And concerning Hūd (عليه السلام), Allāh (عز وجل) said,

﴿ ۞ وَإِلَىٰ عَادٍ أَخَاهُمْ هُودًا ۗ قَالَ يَٰقَوْمِ ٱعْبُدُوا۟ ٱللَّهَ مَا لَكُم مِّنْ إِلَٰهٍ غَيْرُهُۥٓ ۚ أَفَلَا تَتَّقُونَ ﴿٦٥﴾ ﴾

"And to [the people of] ʿĀd, [we have sent] their brother Hūd. He said: O my people, worship Allāh; you have no deity other than Him. Will you not then fear Him?" [Sūrah al-Aʿrāf 7:65]

And concerning Ṣāliḥ (عليه السلام), Allāh (عز وجل) said,

﴿ وَإِلَىٰ ثَمُودَ أَخَاهُمْ صَٰلِحًا ۗ قَالَ يَٰقَوْمِ ٱعْبُدُوا۟ ٱللَّهَ مَا لَكُم مِّنْ إِلَٰهٍ غَيْرُهُۥ ۖ قَدْ جَآءَتْكُم بَيِّنَةٌ مِّن رَّبِّكُمْ ۖ هَٰذِهِۦ نَاقَةُ ٱللَّهِ لَكُمْ ءَايَةً ۖ فَذَرُوهَا تَأْكُلْ فِىٓ أَرْضِ ٱللَّهِ ۖ وَلَا تَمَسُّوهَا بِسُوٓءٍ فَيَأْخُذَكُمْ عَذَابٌ أَلِيمٌ ﴿٧٣﴾ ﴾

"And to [the people of] Thamūd, [we have sent] their brother Ṣāliḥ. He said: O my people, worship Allāh; you have no deity other than Him. Surely, clear evidence has come to you from your Lord. This is the she-camel of Allāh which is a sign for you. So allow it to eat from Allāh's land and do not harm it lest a painful torment should overcome you." [Sūrah al-Aʿrāf 7:73]

And Allāh (ﷻ) said,

﴿ وَإِلَىٰ مَدْيَنَ أَخَاهُمْ شُعَيْبًا ۗ قَالَ يَٰقَوْمِ ٱعْبُدُوا۟ ٱللَّهَ مَا لَكُم مِّنْ إِلَٰهٍ غَيْرُهُۥ ۖ قَدْ جَآءَتْكُم بَيِّنَةٌ مِّن رَّبِّكُمْ ۖ فَأَوْفُوا۟ ٱلْكَيْلَ وَٱلْمِيزَانَ وَلَا تَبْخَسُوا۟ ٱلنَّاسَ أَشْيَآءَهُمْ وَلَا تُفْسِدُوا۟ فِى ٱلْأَرْضِ بَعْدَ إِصْلَٰحِهَا ۚ ذَٰلِكُمْ خَيْرٌ لَّكُمْ إِن كُنتُم مُّؤْمِنِينَ ﴿٨٥﴾ ﴾

"And to [the people of] **Madyan,** [we have sent] **their brother Shuʿayb. He said: O my people, worship Allāh; you have no deity other than Him. Surely, clear evidence has come to you from your Lord. So honour the scale and weigh goods appropriately; and do not deprive people of what they are due. And do not bring corruption to the earth after it has experienced rectification. That is better for you, if you should be Believers."** [Sūrah al-Aʿrāf 7:85]

And concerning Abraham [Ibrāhīm] (عليه السلام), Allāh (ﷻ) said,

﴿ وَإِبْرَٰهِيمَ إِذْ قَالَ لِقَوْمِهِ ٱعْبُدُوا۟ ٱللَّهَ وَٱتَّقُوهُ ۖ ذَٰلِكُمْ خَيْرٌ لَّكُمْ إِن كُنتُمْ تَعْلَمُونَ ﴿١٦﴾ ﴾

"And [remember] **Abraham** (Ibrāhīm)**, when he said to his people: Worship Allāh and fear Him. That is best for you, if you should know."** [Sūrah al-ʿAnkabūt 29:16]

This is exactly what the Messenger of Allāh (ﷺ) did when he sent Muʿādh Ibn Jabal (رضي الله عنه) to the people of Yemen, he said to him, "You are going to a nation from the People of the Book. So let the first thing that you call them to be the *Tawḥīd* of Allāh [to worship Allāh alone without any partners). If they accept that, then inform them that Allāh has obligated upon them five prayers to be performed during their day and night. If they establish the Prayer, then inform them that Allāh has made obligatory upon them *zakāh* which must be taken from their wealth. It is to be taken from their rich and re-distributed amongst the poor from amongst them. And if they obey you in this, then take from them *zakāh* but beware of the most valuable of their wealth."[1]

This is the very reason why Allāh (عَزَّوَجَلَّ) created *al-Jinn* and mankind. He (عَزَّوَجَلَّ) said,

﴿ وَمَا خَلَقْتُ ٱلْجِنَّ وَٱلْإِنسَ إِلَّا لِيَعْبُدُونِ ٥٦ ﴾

"And I [Allāh] did not create the *Jinn* nor mankind except that they should worship Me."

[Sūrah al-Dhāriyāt 51:56]

Those people who call to rectification but base their call to rectification upon a political agenda, economics and financial issues or the redistribution of wealth or the like of this, then these people have engaged in actions that oppose the way of the Messenger (ﷺ) and are thus rejected.

Whoever desires rectification but does not make the establishment of *Tawḥīd* the basis of his call and his goal has certainly opposed the methodology of the Prophets and has abandoned the legislated means of rectification as understood by the people of the *Sunnah* and the *Jamāʿah*.

Look at those who presently claim that they are working towards rectification and even take upon this name. You will find that they severely oppose this principle. The redistribution of wealth is all they discuss day and night, and opposing those in positions of authority is the focal point of their conversations. They have no concern with this

---

[1] Related by al-Bukhārī (no. 7372) and Muslim (no. 19).

measure to begin with except to "throw dust into the eyes" as the saying goes. As for the *Salafīs*, the people of the *Sunnah* and the *Jamāʿah* then they firmly believe that the promise of Allāh is true if they implement Islāmic monotheism (*Tawḥīd*) and worhip Allāh alone.

[They believe that:]

- Allāh will grant them authority in the earth just as He granted it to those who preceded them.
- Allāh will establish them upon the Religion that He is pleased with.
- Allāh will replace their fear with peace and safety.

Allāh (عَزَّوَجَلَّ) said,

﴿ وَعَدَ ٱللَّهُ ٱلَّذِينَ ءَامَنُوا۟ مِنكُمْ وَعَمِلُوا۟ ٱلصَّٰلِحَٰتِ لَيَسْتَخْلِفَنَّهُمْ فِى ٱلْأَرْضِ كَمَا ٱسْتَخْلَفَ ٱلَّذِينَ مِن قَبْلِهِمْ وَلَيُمَكِّنَنَّ لَهُمْ دِينَهُمُ ٱلَّذِى ٱرْتَضَىٰ لَهُمْ وَلَيُبَدِّلَنَّهُم مِّنۢ بَعْدِ خَوْفِهِمْ أَمْنًا ۚ يَعْبُدُونَنِى لَا يُشْرِكُونَ بِى شَيْـًٔا ۚ وَمَن كَفَرَ بَعْدَ ذَٰلِكَ فَأُو۟لَٰٓئِكَ هُمُ ٱلْفَٰسِقُونَ ﴿٥٥﴾ ﴾

"Allāh has promised those who believe among you, and do righteous good deeds, that He will certainly grant them authority in the earth, just as He granted it to those before them, and He will establish them upon their Religion, which He has chosen for them [i.e. Islām**]. And He will surely replace their fear with safety [**provided**] they worship Me while not associating anything with Me. But whoever disbelieves after this then they are the rebelliously disobedient."**

[Sūrah an-Nūr 24:55][1]

[1] **Translator's Note:** Imām al-Sa'dī (d.1376H) said in *Taysīr al-Karīm al-Raḥmān* (p. 521) in explanation of this *āyah*, "This is one of His true promises whose meaning and accomplishment has been witnessed. He promised those who came with *īmān* (true faith) and righteous and correct actions from this *Ummah* that He would cause them to be successors upon the earth, so that they are the ones in authority and in charge of the affairs. Further that He would establish their Religion, that which He was pleased with for them, which is the Religion of Islām which gained ascendancy over all of the religions. He was pleased with it for this *Ummah*, due to its excellency, nobility and His favours upon it, and He enabled them to establish it and to establish its laws and prescriptions, relating both to manifest and non-manifest matters, upon themselves and others, due to the people of the other religions and the rest of the disbelievers being conquered and humbled.
He would change their condition of fear to one of security, since it was previously the case that one of them would not be able to manifest his Religion, and they suffered harm and injury from the disbelievers. The united body of the Muslims was very small in number in comparison to the rest and the people of the earth combined to attack them and to hope for their downfall.
So Allāh promised them these things when the verse was sent down at a time when they did not witness ascendancy and establishment upon the earth, nor the ability to fully establish the Religion of Islām and full security such as would enable them to worship Allāh, not associating anything with Him, in a state of not having fear of anyone except Allāh.
The first and foremost part of this *Ummah* combined *īmān* and righteous action to a degree surpassing everyone else, so He established them in the land and gave them authority over the people, and granted them the conquest of the East and the West. They attained full security and complete authority and establishment, so this is one of the astounding signs of Allāh.
This applies until the Hour is established. Whenever this nation combines *īmān* and righteous action, then that which Allāh promised will certainly occur.

The Second Measure
Rectification Starts with the Individual and it does not Start with the Community, nor the Leader or Other than Him - in Reality each Person Should Start with their Own Self then those who are Closest to Them and then Those who are Closest to Them

Allāh (ﷻ) said,

﴿ إِنَّ ٱللَّهَ لَا يُغَيِّرُ مَا بِقَوۡمٍ حَتَّىٰ يُغَيِّرُواْ مَا بِأَنفُسِهِمۡۗ وَإِذَآ أَرَادَ ٱللَّهُ بِقَوۡمٖ سُوٓءٗا فَلَا مَرَدَّ لَهُۥۚ وَمَا لَهُم مِّن دُونِهِۦ مِن وَالٍ ﴿١١﴾ ﴾

"Indeed, Allāh will not change the condition of a people until they change what is within themselves. And when Allāh wants to punish a people, there is nothing that can repel it and they will find besides Him no protector." [Sūrah al-Raʿd 13:11]

So the starting point is with one's self then those who are closest and then those who are closest.

Allāh (ﷻ) said,

﴿ وَأَنذِرۡ عَشِيرَتَكَ ٱلۡأَقۡرَبِينَ ﴿٢١٤﴾ ﴾

"And warn your tribe of near kindred."
[Sūrah al-Shuʿarāʾ 26:214]

Abū Hurayrah (رضي الله عنه) narrated that the Messenger of Allāh (ﷺ) said, "Give charity." Then the man responded, "O Messenger of Allāh (ﷺ), I possess a *dīnār*." Then he [the Messenger of Allāh (ﷺ)] said, "Give it as charity to yourself." Then he said, "I have another." Then he [the Messenger of

Allāh (ﷺ)] said, "Give it as charity to your wife." Then he said, "I have another." Then he [the Messenger of Allāh (ﷺ)] said, "Give it as charity to your child." Then he said, "I have another." Then he [the Messenger of Allāh (ﷺ)] said, "Give it as charity to your servant." Then he said, "I have another." Then he [the Messenger of Allāh (ﷺ)] said, "You know best what to do with it."[1]

If this is the case in matters of charity, then what do you think is the case when it pertains to rectification!

The path of rectification starts with the individual.

The rectification of the individual leads to the rectification of the family.

The rectification of the family leads to the rectification of the neighborhood.

The rectification of the neighborhood leads to the rectification of the region. The rectification of the region leads to the rectification of the country. The rectification of the country leads to the rectification of this nation. The rectification of this nation leads to the rectification of the entire world. So beginning with oneself is the foundation.

إبْدَأْ بِنَفْسِكَ فَنْهَـــهَا عَنْ غيِّهَا   فَإِذَا انْـــتَهَتْ عَنْهُ فَأَنْتَ حَكِيمُ

Start with your own soul and prevent it from its transgression,
If it ceases from that, then you are truly wise.

◆◆❖◆◆

[1] Related by al-Nisā'ī (no. 2535) and Abū Dāwūd (no. 1691). This *ḥadīth* is sound.

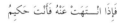

The Third Measure
Knowledge Precedes Speech and Actions

Al-Bukhārī (d.256H) entitled a chapter in his *Ṣaḥīḥ* in *Kitāb al-ʿIlm*, (Chapter: Knowledge precedes speech and action due to the saying of Allāh,

﴿ فَٱعْلَمْ أَنَّهُۥ لَآ إِلَـٰهَ إِلَّا ٱللَّهُ ﴾

> **"Know that none has the right to be worshipped except Allāh."** [Sūrah Muḥammad 47:19]

So He [Allāh] began with knowledge. The Scholars are the inheritors of the Prophets. The Prophets left behind knowledge and whoever takes from it has taken a handsome share. Whoever sets out upon a path in search of knowledge Allāh will make easy for him a path towards Paradise.

And Allāh (ﷻ) said,

﴿ إِنَّمَا يَخْشَى ٱللَّهَ مِنْ عِبَادِهِ ٱلْعُلَمَـٰٓؤُا۟ ﴾

> **"It is only those who have knowledge among His servants that fear Allāh."** [Sūrah Fāṭir 35:28]

And He said,

﴿ وَمَا يَعْقِلُهَآ إِلَّا ٱلْعَـٰلِمُونَ ﴾

> **"And none will understand them except the people of knowledge."** [Sūrah al-ʿAnkabūt 29:43]

And He says,

﴿ وَقَالُوا۟ لَوْ كُنَّا نَسْمَعُ أَوْ نَعْقِلُ مَا كُنَّا فِىٓ أَصْحَـٰبِ ٱلسَّعِيرِ ﴿١٠﴾ ﴾

> **"And they will say: If only we had listened or contemplated, we would not be from among the people of the blazing Fire."** [Sūrah al-Mulk 67:10]

And He said,

﴿ هَلْ يَسْتَوِى ٱلَّذِينَ يَعْلَمُونَ وَٱلَّذِينَ لَا يَعْلَمُونَ ﴾

> **"Are those who know equal to those who do not?"** [Sūrah az-Zumar 39:9]

The Prophet (ﷺ) said, "Whomever Allāh wants good for, He grants him understanding of the Religion." And he (ﷺ) said, "Knowledge is aquired through learning."

Abū Dharr (رضي الله عنه) said, "If you were to place a sword upon this -and he pointed towards the back of his neck- and then I thought that I could utter a word that I heard from the Prophet (ﷺ) before you were able to strike me, then I would say it."

Ibn ʿAbbās said, "[The statement of Allāh] **'Be *rabbāniyūn*,'** means to be religious Scholars who are patient and wise. The term *rabbānī* is applied to one who cultivates the people and teaches them the smaller issues of knowledge before the larger ones.")[1]

The Religion is built upon two foundations:

1. That we do not worship anything except Allāh.

---

[1] Related by al-Bukhārī, The Book Of Knowledge, Chapter: Knowledge Precedes Speech and Actions.

2. That we do not worhip Allāh except in the manner that He has legislated.

The meaning of this measure is that it is upon the one who is calling to rectification to analyse closely that which he says and does to the extent that he is certain of his [speech and actions]. So that whatever transpires from him is based upon certainty of conviction that is based on textual evidence.

No one should set out upon a path that he claims is the path of rectification unless he knows that it is something that has been legislated by Allāh (ﷻ). He should never oppose the *Sunnah* in this.

He does not stand up upon a pulpit and criticize the Muslim leaders, claiming that this brings about rectification because this opposes what the Messenger (ﷺ) has commanded us with.

ʿIyāḍ Ibn Ghunm (رضي الله عنه) narrated that the Messenger of Allāh (ﷺ) said, "Whoever wishes to sincerely advise a person in authority should not expose this publicly. Rather, he should take him by the hand and go into seclusion with him. If he accepts this from him then this is one thing, and if not then he has fulfilled the duty that was upon him."[1]

Similarly, no one should use demonstrations as a way to bring about rectification because this action was not from the *Sunnah* of the Messenger (ﷺ) nor was it from the *Sunnah* of the pious predecessors (*al-Salaf al-Ṣāliḥ*).

Thus, a person should not speak or act except with knowledge as knowledge precedes statements and actions.

◆◆❖◆◆

[1] Related by Aḥmad (3/ 403) and Ibn Abī ʿĀṣim in the book *al-Sunnah* (2 /737, no. 1130). The individual that checked Ibn Abī ʿĀṣim, Assistant Professor Bāsim al-Jawābirah, said, "Its chain is authentic."

The Fourth Measure His Knowledge Should be in Accordance to The Understanding of the Pious Predecessors (*al-Salaf al-Ṣāliḥ*)

Muʿāwiyah Ibn Abī Sufyān (ﷺ) stood up amongst us and said, "Indeed, the Messenger of Allāh (ﷺ) stood up before us and said, 'Verily, those who preceded you from the people of the book divided into seventy-two sects; and this nation will divide into seventy-three sects. Seventy-two of these sects will inhabit the Hellfire while one will be in Paradise. That one sect is the *Jamāʿah*.'"[1]

There is no safety in following any methodology unless it is the methodology of the *Jamāʿah*.

This is the way of the Believers as Allāh (ﷻ) said,

﴿ وَمَن يُشَاقِقِ ٱلرَّسُولَ مِنۢ بَعْدِ مَا تَبَيَّنَ لَهُ ٱلْهُدَىٰ وَيَتَّبِعْ غَيْرَ سَبِيلِ
ٱلْمُؤْمِنِينَ نُوَلِّهِۦ مَا تَوَلَّىٰ وَنُصْلِهِۦ جَهَنَّمَ ۖ وَسَآءَتْ مَصِيرًا ﴿١١٥﴾ ﴾

> **"And whoever opposes the Messenger after guidance has been made clear to him, and follows other than the way of the believers; We will direct him towards the path which he has chosen, and burn him in Hell - and what an evil destination."** [Sūrah an-Nisāʾ4:115]

---

[1] Related by Aḥmad in his *Musnad* (4/102), Abū Dāwūd (no. 4597), al-Ājurrī in his book *al-Sharʿiyyah* (checked edition, 1/132). This narration is authenticated due to supporting narrations (*ṣaḥīḥ li ghayrhi*), and some alluded to the possibility of it being *mutawātir*. This narration has also been authenticated by the one who performed the checking of the book *Jāmiʿ al-Uṣūl* (10/32) and by al-Albānī in his *Silsilah al-Aḥādīth al-Ṣaḥīḥah* (no. 204). Al-Albānī also mentioned a number of narrations that provide further textual support for this narration. Refer to *Naẓm al-Mutanāthir min al-Ḥadīth al-Mutawātir* (p. 32-34).

Whoever desires to attain knowledge should adhere to the way of the believers and he should not follow in the footsteps of the people of differing and sectarianism from those sects that oppose that which the Messenger (ﷺ) and his Companions (رضي الله عنهم) were upon.

These are the guidelines for rectification, which if anyone was to oppose from those who claim to be proponents of rectification then they are considered to be amongst those who spread corruption.

Allāh (سبحانه وتعالى) said,

﴿ وَإِذَا قِيلَ لَهُمْ لَا تُفْسِدُوا۟ فِى ٱلْأَرْضِ قَالُوٓا۟ إِنَّمَا نَحْنُ مُصْلِحُونَ ۝١١ أَلَآ إِنَّهُمْ هُمُ ٱلْمُفْسِدُونَ وَلَـٰكِن لَّا يَشْعُرُونَ ۝١٢ ﴾

> "And when it is said to them, 'Do not cause corruption in the earth,' they say, 'We are only people of rectification.' Indeed, they are the ones who spread corruption, but they do not realize it."
>
> [Sūrah al-Baqarah 2:11-12]

◆◆❖◆◆

The Fifth Measure
To Adorn Oneself when Calling [to Allāh] with the Attributes that have been Described in the *Qur'ān*, the Prophetic *Ḥadīth* and in the Narrations of the *Salaf*

The following are some of those evidences:

Allāh (ﷻ) said,

﴿ قُلۡ هَٰذِهِۦ سَبِيلِيٓ أَدۡعُوٓاْ إِلَى ٱللَّهِۚ عَلَىٰ بَصِيرَةٍ أَنَا۠ وَمَنِ ٱتَّبَعَنِيۖ وَسُبۡحَٰنَ ٱللَّهِ وَمَآ أَنَا۠ مِنَ ٱلۡمُشۡرِكِينَ ١٠٨ ﴾

"Say: This is my way; I invite unto Allāh with insight; myself and those who follow me. And glorified is Allāh; and I am not from those who direct worship to other than Him." [Sūrah Yūsuf 12:108]

Allāh (ﷻ) said,

﴿ ٱدۡعُ إِلَىٰ سَبِيلِ رَبِّكَ بِٱلۡحِكۡمَةِ وَٱلۡمَوۡعِظَةِ ٱلۡحَسَنَةِۖ وَجَٰدِلۡهُم بِٱلَّتِي هِيَ أَحۡسَنُۚ إِنَّ رَبَّكَ هُوَ أَعۡلَمُ بِمَن ضَلَّ عَن سَبِيلِهِۦۖ وَهُوَ أَعۡلَمُ بِٱلۡمُهۡتَدِينَ ١٢٥ ﴾

"Call to the way of your Lord with wisdom and good admonition; and argue with them in a manner which is better. Certainly, your Lord is the most knowledgeable concerning who has strayed from His path and He is the most knowledgeable concerning whom is guided." [Sūrah al-Naḥl 16:125]

Allāh (ﷻ) said,

﴿ يَٰبُنَيَّ أَقِمِ ٱلصَّلَوٰةَ وَأۡمُرۡ بِٱلۡمَعۡرُوفِ وَٱنۡهَ عَنِ ٱلۡمُنكَرِ وَٱصۡبِرۡ عَلَىٰ مَآ أَصَابَكَۖ إِنَّ ذَٰلِكَ مِنۡ عَزۡمِ ٱلۡأُمُورِ ١٧ ﴾

> **"O my son! Establish the prayer, enjoin the good, and forbid the evil, and endure with patience whatever afflicts you. Certainly, These are from the most important of matters."** [Sūrah Luqmān 31:17]

ʿĀʾishah, the wife of the Prophet (ﷺ), narrated that the Messenger of Allāh (ﷺ) said, "O ʿĀʾishah, certainly Allāh is gentle and He loves gentleness and He gives as a result of gentleness what He does not give because of harshness or anything other than it." [Agreed upon]

Saʿīd Ibn Abī Burdah said upon the authority of his father who narrated from his father [the grandfather of Saʿīd Ibn Abī Burdah] that the Prophet (ﷺ) said to Muʿādh and Abū Mūsá as he sent them to Yemen, "Make things easy for the people and do not make things difficult, and give glad tidings and do not chase them away. Be cooperative and do not differ." [Agreed upon]

It becomes clear from these textual evidences that the essential attributes that every caller (*dāʿiyah*) must exhibit is:

1. **The First Attribute:** Knowledge and understanding of what he is calling to, what he is commanding and what he is prohibiting.
2. **The Second Attribute:** That gentleness is observed when inviting the people, when commanding them with good and when forbidding them from evil. Allāh (ﷻ) said about His Messenger (ﷺ),

﴿ فَبِمَا رَحْمَةٍ مِّنَ ٱللَّهِ لِنتَ لَهُمْ ۖ وَلَوْ كُنتَ فَظًّا غَلِيظَ ٱلْقَلْبِ لَٱنفَضُّوا۟ مِنْ حَوْلِكَ ۖ فَٱعْفُ عَنْهُمْ وَٱسْتَغْفِرْ لَهُمْ وَشَاوِرْهُمْ فِى ٱلْأَمْرِ ۖ فَإِذَا عَزَمْتَ فَتَوَكَّلْ عَلَى ٱللَّهِ ۚ إِنَّ ٱللَّهَ يُحِبُّ ٱلْمُتَوَكِّلِينَ ﴿١٥٩﴾ ﴾

> **"By the mercy of Allāh** [O Muḥammad]**, you were lenient with them. And if you had been stern and harsh of heart, they would have disbanded from around you. So excuse them and seek forgiveness for them and consult them in the matter. Then once you have made a decision, then rely upon Allāh. Indeed, Allāh loves those who rely upon Him."** [Sūrah Āli-ʿImrān 3:159]

3. **The Third Attribute:** Forebearance after having called the people. He should not be hasty or become angry, and he should suppress his anger.
4. **The Fourth Attribute:** Being patient after calling the people. Surely those who call the people to the way of Allāh are often subjected to harm as a result of their call so it upon them to be paitient.

Ibn Taymiyyah (d.728H) said, "Promoting the *Sunnah* and forbidding innovation (*bidʿah*) is considered to be commanding the good and forbidding evil and it is amongst the best of the righteous deeds. It is obligatory that this is done seeking the pleasure of Allāh and in accordance to what has been commanded. In the narration it is found that whoever enjoins the good and forbids the evil must be:

- Knowledgeable concerning what he is commanding and forbidding.
- Gentle in his attempt to enjoin the good and forbid the evil.
- Forebearing when enjoining [the good] and forbidding [the evil].

Knowledge precedes the command, gentleness accompanies it and forebearance follows it. If this individual was not knowledgeable, then it would be inappropriate for him to take a stance upon an issue of which he has no knowledge.

If he was knowledgeable but not gentle then he would be like the doctor who lacks gentleness and is harsh with the sick, and this would not be tolerated from him. It is also similar to the educator who is rough and as such children do not benefit from him.

Allāh (ﷻ) said to Mūsā and Hārūn,

﴿ فَقُولَا لَهُۥ قَوْلًا لَّيِّنًا لَّعَلَّهُۥ يَتَذَكَّرُ أَوْ يَخْشَىٰ ﴿٤٤﴾ ﴾

> **"And speak to him gently so that perhaps he may accept the admonition or fear** [Allāh]**."**
> [Sūrah Ṭā Ha 20:44]

Whenever someone enjoins the good and forbids the evil, they are likely to be harmed so they should be patient and forebearing.

As Allāh (ﷻ) said,

﴿ يَـٰبُنَيَّ أَقِمِ ٱلصَّلَوٰةَ وَأْمُرْ بِٱلْمَعْرُوفِ وَٱنْهَ عَنِ ٱلْمُنكَرِ وَٱصْبِرْ عَلَىٰ
مَآ أَصَابَكَ ۖ إِنَّ ذَٰلِكَ مِنْ عَزْمِ ٱلْأُمُورِ ﴿١٧﴾ ﴾

> **"O my son! Establish the prayer, enjoin the good, and forbid the evil, and endure with patience whatever afflicts you. Certainly, These are from the most important of matters."** [Sūrah Luqmān 31:17]

Allāh has commanded His Prophet with paitience upon the harm of the idolators in various places [throughout the *Qur'ān*] and he is without doubt the Imām [leader and example] of those who enjoin the good and forbid the evil."[1]

Ibn Taymiyyah (d.728H) also said, "Gentleness is the path to enjoin the good and forbid the evil, and that is why it is said, 'Let your enjoinment of good be good and let your forbiddance of evil not be evil.'"[2]

◆◆❖◆◆

---

[1] Refer to *Minhāj al-Sunnah al-Nabawiyyah* (5/254-255) of Ibn Taymiyyah.

[2] Refer to *al-Istiqāmah* (2/210-211). Also compare this passage to what is found in *Majmū' al-Fatāwā* (28/126).

Conclusion

I will close with some words which are an encouragement to adhere to the *Sunnah* and learn the Religion, and these words are from the speech of the Imāms.

It is narrated upon Abū al-ʿĀliyah (d.90H) that he said, "Learn Islām, and if you learn it do not turn away from it. Stick to the Straight Path for verily it is Islām. And do not deviate from this path, to the right or to the left. It is likewise incumbent upon you to adhere to the *Sunnah* of your Prophet (ﷺ) and that which his Companions were upon."

And in a version of this narration collected by al-Ājurrī, "The *Sunnah* of his Companions before a group that appeared in their midst killed [this] Companion and before they did what they did. We read the *Qur'ān* fifteen years before they killed this Companion and before they did what they did. Beware of these desires which inspire enmity and hatred between the people."[1]

Al-Shāfiʿī (رحمه الله) said, "Whoever studies the *Qur'ān* becomes of great worth. Whoever speaks regarding jurisprudence (*fiqh*) his stature will be raised. Whoever writes down *ḥadīth* his arguments become strong. Whoever studies arithmetic will aquire firm judgement and intelligence. Whoever does not protect himself will not benefit from his knowledge."[2]

Ibn Ḥibbān (رحمه الله) said, "In adhering to his *Sunnah* (ﷺ) lies complete security and an assortment of virtue and nobility. Its light will never be extinguished and its evidence will never be disproven. Whoever adheres to it is safe and whoever opposes it is blamed. This is because it

---

[1] This narration is authentic. It was collected by Ibn Waḍḍāḥ in *al-Bidaʿ wa al-Nahī ʿanhā* (p. 39) and declared authentic by the individual who provided the checking for *Miftāḥ al-Jannah* - may Allāh grant him success - (p. 138); and by al-Ājurrī in *al-Sharīʿah* (1/124, no. 19) and it was also declared authentic by the individual who checked this book; and by Ibn Baṭṭah in his book, *al-Ibānah* (1/ 299 & 338, no. 136, 202) with a shorter wording that is similar.

[2] Refer to *Siyar Aʿlām al-Nubalāʾ* (10/24) of al-Dhahabī.

is a fortified stronghold and a pillar of support whose virtues are evident and whose rope is firm.

Whoever adheres to it will prevail, and whoever desires other than it will perish. Those who cling to it are from the people of happiness and bliss in the hereafter and people who are envied in this life."[1]

This completes this conclusion and it brings the book to a close. All praise is due to Allāh, who by His blessings and favour, righteous actions are accomplished. Glory is to You, O Allah, and praise is to You. I bear witness that there is none worthy of worship but You. I seek Your forgiveness and repent to You. Send praise, O Allāh, upon Muḥammad and upon the family of Muḥammad just as you bestowed your praise upon Abraham [Ibrāhīm] and upon the family of Abraham [Ibrāhīm]. Indeed, You are Praiseworthy, Most Glorious. O Allāh, bless Muḥammad and the family of Muhammad as you have blessed Abraham [Ibrāhīm] and the family of Abraham [Ibrāhīm]. Indeed, You are are Praiseworthy, Most Glorious.

تم بحمد الله

[1] Refer to *Ṣaḥīḥ Ibn Ḥibbān* (*al-Iḥsān*, 1/86).

Glossary

A

Āyah: (pl. *āyāt*) "sign," a verse of the *Qur'ān*.
Āhād: a narration which has not reached the level of *mutawātir*.
Ahādīth: see *hadīth*.
'Alayhis-salām: "may Allāh (ﷻ) protect and preserve him." It is said after the name of a Prophet of Allāh or after the name of an Angel.
Ansār: "helpers;" the Muslims of al-Madīnah who supported the Muslims who migrated from Makkah.
'Arsh: Throne of Allāh (ﷻ).
'Asr: the afternoon Prayer.
Awliyā': see *Walī*.

B

Bid'ah: Heresy (any innovatory practice).
Burāq: An animal bigger than a donkey and smaller than a horse on which the Prophet (ﷺ) went for the *Mi'rāj*.

D

Dā'ī: one engaged in *da'wah*, caller.
Da'aef: "weak," unauthentic narration.
Da'wah: invitation, call to Allāh (ﷻ).
Dīn: a completed way of life prescribed by Allāh (ﷻ).
Dhikr: (pl. *adhkār*) remembrance of Allāh (ﷻ) with the heart, sayings of the tongue and actions of our limbs.

E

Īmān: faith, to affirm all that was revealed to the Prophet.

F

Fāhish: one who talks evil.
Fard Kifāyah: collective obligation - if fulfilled by a part of the community then the rest are not obligated.
Fatwā: (pl. *fatāwā*) religious verdicts.
Faqīh: A Scholar who can give religious verdicts.
Fiqh: Islāmic jurisprudence, understanding.
Fitnah: (pl. *fitan*) Trials, persecution, conflicts and strifes.
Fitrah: the natural disposition that one is born upon.

G

Ghulū: going to an extreme.
Ghusl: A ceremonial bath necessary for the one who is in a state of *Janābah*.

H

Hadīth: (pl. *ahādīh*) the saying, actions and approvals narrated from the Prophet (ﷺ).
Halāl: lawful.
Hanīf: pure Islāmic Monotheism (worshipping Allāh alone and nothing else).
Harām: unlawful and forbidden.
Hasan: fine, good; a term used for an authentic *hadīth*, which does not reach the level of *Sahīh*.
Harj: killing.
Al-Harūriyyah: an especially un-orthodox religious sect that branched off from the *Khawārij*.
Hijrah: migration from the land of *Shirk* to the land of Islām.

Hukm: a judgment of legal decision (especially of Allāh).

I

'Ibādah: worship, worship of Allāh.
Ihsān: worshipping Allāh as though you see Him. However, since you cannot see Him, then know that He sees you.
Ijmā': consensus, a unified opinion of Scholars regarding a certain issue.
Ijtihād: exertion of effort; the process of arriving at a reasoned decision by a Scholar on an issue.
Imām: leaders; leaders in Prayer, knowledge in *fiqh*, leader of a state.
Isnād: the chain of narrators linking the collector of the saying to the person quoted.
Istikhārah: a Prayer consisting of two units (*rak'ah*) asking Allāh for guidance.
Istiwā: ascending; the ascending of Allāh above the Throne (in the manner that befits His Majesty).

J

Janābah: state of a person after having sexual intercourse or sexual discharge.
Janāzah: (pl. *janā'iz*): Funeral.
Jihād: striving, struggling, fighting to make the Word of Allāh supreme.
Jumu'ah: Friday.
Jinn: invisible creation, created by Allāh from smokeless fire.
Junub: a person who is in the state of *janābah*.

K

Ka'bah: a square stone building in *al-Masjidul-Haram* (the great mosque in Makkah which Muslims go to for pilgrimage and which all Muslims direct their face in Prayer).
Al-Kabā'ir: the major sins.
Khārijī: (pl. *Khawārij*): those who declared that a Muslim becomes a disbeliever due to committing a major sin alone.

Khalīfah: (pl. *khulafā'*): the head of the Islāmic government to whom the oath of allegiance is given.
Khilāfah: an Islāmic state.
Khutbah: (person *khatīb)*, religious talk (sermon).
Kufr: (person *kāfir)* act of disbelief in the Religion of Islām.

M

Madhhab: position or opinion of a scholar; school of Islāmic Jurisprudence.
Makrūh: not approved of, undesirable from the point of view of Religion, although not punishable.
Manhaj: way; method; methodology.
Marfū': raised; a narration attributed to the Prophet (ﷺ).
Masjid: mosque.
Mawbiqāt: great destructive sins.
Mudallis: one who practises *tadlīs.*
Muhājir: (pl. *muhājirūn, muhājirīn*) one who migrated from the land of the disbelievers to the land of the Muslims for the sake of Allāh.
Muhaddith: scholar of the science of *hadīth.*
Muftī: one who gives *fatāwā.*
Mujāhid: (pl. *mujāhidūn*): a Muslim warrior in *Jihād.*
Mujtahid: one who is qualified to pass judgment using *ijtihād.*
Munkar: "rejected;" a narration which is un-authentic itself and contradicts and authentic narrations.
Muqallid: one who practices *taqlīd.*
Mushrik: (pl. *mushrikūn*) polytheists, pagans and disbelievers in the oneness of Allāh (ﷻ) and His Messenger (ﷺ).
Mustahabb: recommended; an action if left it is not punishable and if done it is rewardable.
Muttaqūn: those who are pious.
Mutawātir: a *hadīth* which is narrated by a very large number of reporters, such that it cannot be supported that they all agreed upon a lie.
Muwahhid: (pl. *muwahhidūn*) one who unifies all of his worship and directs it to Allāh alone.
Mawdū': fabricated; spurious; invented (narration).

Mawqūf: stopped; a narration from a Companion (not going back to the Prophet (ﷺ)).
Mawsūl: "connected;" a continuous *isnād* (can be narrated back to the Prophet (ﷺ)).

N

Nāfilah: (pl. *nawāfil*) Optional practice of worship.
Niyyah: intention from the heart.
Nusuk: a sacrifice.

Q

Qadar: Divine pre-ordainment; that which Allāh has ordained for his creation.
Qiblah: the direction the Muslims face during Prayer.
Qiyās: analogical deduction of Islāmic laws. New laws are deduced from old laws based upon similarity between their causes.
Qunūt: "devotion;" a special supplication while standing in the Prayer.
Quraysh: one of the greatest tribes in Arabia in the pre-Islāmic period of Ignorance. The Prophet (ﷺ) belonged to this tribe.

R

Rāfidī: the correct title for the extreme *Shī'ah.* Those who bear malice and grudges against the noble Companions to the extent that they declare them to be apostates. They also hold that the *Qur'ān* which the Muslims have is neither complete nor preserved from corruption.
Ramadān: the ninth month of Islāmic calendar, in which Muslims observe fasting.

S

Sahābah: Muslims who met the Prophet (ﷺ) believing in him and died believing in him.
Sahīh: authentic, the highest rank of classification of authentic *ahādīth.*
Salaf/Salafus-Sālihīn: pious predecessors; the Muslims of the first three generations: the companions, the successors and their successors.
Salafī: one who ascribes oneself to the *salaf* and follows their way.
Sīrah: the life story of the Prophet (ﷺ).
Sharī'ah: the divine code of law of Islām.
Shawwāl: the month after *Ramadān.*
Shaytān: Satan
Shī'ah: (see *Rāfidī*) a collective name for various sects claiming love for *Ahlul-Bayt.*
Shirk: associating partners with Allāh directly or indirectly; compromising any aspects of *Tawhīd.*
Sūrah: a chapter of the *Qur'ān*
Sunnah: "example, practice;" the way of life of the Prophet (ﷺ), consisting of his words, actions and silent approvals. The *Sunnah* is contained in various *ahādīth.*

T

Tābi'ī: (pl. *tābi'īn*) the generation after the Companions of the Prophet (ﷺ).
Tafsīr: explanation of the *Qur'ān.*
Tāghūt: anything worshiped other than the real God (Allāh) (i.e. false deities).
Tahajjud: voluntary, recommended Prayer between the compulsory prayers of *'Ishā'* and *Fajr.*
Takhrīj: to reference a *hadīth* to its sources and analyze its i*snāds.*
Taqlīd: blind following; to follow someone's opinion (*madhhab*) without evidence.
Taqwā: acting in obedience to Allāh, hoping for His mercy upon light from Him and *taqwā* is leaving acts of disobedience, out of fear of Him, upon light from Him.

Tarjamah: notes about a reporter of *hadīth.*
Tawwāf: the circumambulation of the *ka'bah.*
Tawhīd: Islāmic Monotheism. The Oneness of Allāh. Believing and acting upon His Lordship, His rights of Worship and Names and Attributes.

U

Uhud: A well known mountain in al-Madīnah. One of the greatest battles in Islāmic history came at its foot. This is called *Ghazwah Uhud.*
'Ulamā': (singular: *'ālim*) scholars.
Umm: mother of, used as an identification.
Ummah: "nation", the Muslims as a whole.
'Umrah: a visit to Makkah during which one performs the *tawwāf* around the *Ka'bah* and the *Sa'ī* between *as-Safā* and *al-Marwah.* It is called the lesser *Hajj.*
Usūl: the fundamentals.

W

Wahyī: the revelation or inspiration of Allāh to His Prophets.
Wahdatul-Wujūd: the belief that everything in existence is infact Allāh. This deviant belief is held by many *Sūfīs.*
Wakīl: disposer of affairs.
Witr: "odd;" the last Prayer at the night, which consists of odd number of *raka'āt* (units).
Walīmah: the wedding feast.
Wasīlah: the means of approach or achieving His closeness to Allāh by getting His favours.
Wudū': an ablution (ritual washing) that is performed before Prayer and other kinds of worship.

Y

Yaqīn: perfect absolute faith.
Yathrib: one of the names of al-Madīnah.

Z

Zakāt: charity that is obligatory on everyone who has wealth over and above a certain limit over which a year has passed (2.5% of saved wealth).
Zakātul-Fitr: an obligatory charity by the Muslims to be given to the poor before the Prayer of *'Īdul-Fitr*.
Zamzam: the sacred water inside the *haram* (the grand mosque) at Makkah.
Zanādiqah: atheists, heretics.

Our Call to the Ummah[1]

[1]: We believe in Allāh and His Names and Attributes, as they were mentioned in the Book of Allāh and in the *Sunnah* of the Messenger of Allāh (ﷺ), without *tahrīf* (distortion), nor *ta'wīl* (figurative interpretation), nor *tamthīl* (making a likeness), nor *tashbīh* (resemblance), nor *ta'tīl* (denial).

[2]: We love the Companions (رضي الله عنهم) of the Messenger of Allāh (ﷺ), and we hate those who speak against them. We believe that to speak ill of them is to speak ill of the Religion, because they are the ones who conveyed it to us. And we love the Family of the Prophet (ﷺ) with love that is permitted by the *Sharī'ah*. 'Imrān Ibn Husayn (رضي الله عنه) said, "O people! Learn the knowledge of the Religion from us, if you do not do so, then you will certainly be misguided."[2]

[3]: We love the People of *Hadīth* and all of the *Salaf* of the *Ummah* from *Ahlus-Sunnah*. Imām Shātibī (d.790H) - رحمه الله - said, "The *Salafus-Sālih*, the Companions, the *tābi'īn* and their successors knew the *Qur'ān*, its sciences and its meanings the best."[3]

[4]: We despise *'ilmul-kalām* (knowledge of theological rhetoric), and we view it to be from amongst the greatest reasons for the division in the *Ummah*.

[5]: We do not accept anything from the Books of *fiqh* (jurisprudence), nor from the Books of *tafsīr* (explanation of the *Qur'ān*), nor from the ancient stories, nor from the *Sīrah* (biography) of the Prophet (ﷺ), except that which has been confirmed from Allāh or from His Messenger (ﷺ). We do not mean that we have rejected them, nor do we claim that we are not in need of them. Rather, we benefit from the

[1] This explanation of our call has bīn summarized from *Tarjumah Abī 'Abdur-Rahmān Muqbil Ibn Hādī al-Wādi'ī* (p. 135-142) of Muqbil Ibn Hādī with minor additions from other sources.
[2] Refer to *al-Kifāyah* (p. 15) of al-Khatīb al-Baghdādī.
[3] Refer to *al-Muwāfiqāt* (2/79) of ash-Shātibī.

discoveries of our Scholars and the jurists and other than them. However, we do not accept a ruling, except with an authentic proof.

[6]: We do not write in our Books, nor do we cover in our lessons, nor do we give sermons with anything except the *Qur'ān*, or the authentic and authoritative *hadīth*. And we detest what emanates from many Books and admonishers in terms of false stories and weak and fabricated *ahādīth*. 'Abdullāh Ibnul-Mubārak (d.181H) - ﷺ - said, "The authentic *ahādīth* are sufficient and the weak *ahādīth* are not needed."[1]

[7]: We do not perform *takfīr* upon any Muslim due to any sin, except *Shirk* with Allāh, or the abandonment of Prayer, or apostasy. We seek refuge in Allāh from that.

[8]: We believe that the *Qur'ān* is the Speech of Allāh, it is not created.

[9]: We hold that our 'obligation is to co-operate with the group that traverses the methodology of the Book and the *Sunnah*, and what the *Salaf* of the *Ummah* were upon; in terms of calling to Allāh the Glorified, and being sincere in worship of Him, and warning from *Shirk*, innovations, and disobedience, and to advise all of the groups that oppose this.'[2] 'So co-operating upon righteousness and piety (*taqwā*) and mutual advising necessitates warning against evil and not co-operating with the wicked.'[3]

[10]: We do not deem it correct to revolt against the Muslim rulers as long as they are Muslims, nor do we feel that revolutions bring about reconciliation. Rather, they corrupt the community.

[11]: We hold that this multiplicity of present day parties is a reason for the division of the Muslims and their weakness. So therefore we set

---

[1] Refer to *al-Jāmi' li-Akhlāqir-Rāwī* (2/159) of as-Suyūtī.

[2] From a *fatwā* by the Committī of Major Scholars dated: 11/16/1417, (no. 18870). It was signed by al-'Allāmah 'Abdul-'Azīz Ibn Bāz, Shaykh 'Abdul-'Azīz Ibn 'Abdullāh ālush-Shaykh, Shaykh 'Abdullāh Ibn 'Abdur-Rahmān al-Ghudayyān, Shaykh Bakr Ibn 'Abdullāh Abū Zayd, and Shaykh Sālih Ibn Fawzān al-Fawzān.

[3] From the words of Shaykh Ibn Bāz in *al-Furqān* magazine (issue no. 14, p. 15).

about 'freeing the minds from the fetters of blind-following and the darkness of sectarianism and party spirit.'[1]

[12]: We restrict our understanding of the Book of Allāh and of the *Sunnah* of the Messenger of Allāh (ﷺ) to the understanding of the *Salaf* of the *Ummah* from the Scholars of *hadīth*, not the blind-followers of their individuals. Rather, we take the truth from wherever it comes. And we know that there are those who claim *Salafiyyah*, yet *Salafiyyah* is free from them, since they bring to the society what Allāh has prohibited. We believe in 'cultivating the young generation upon this Islām, purified from all that we have mentioned, giving to them a correct Islamic education from the start - without any influence from the disbelieving western education.'[2]

[13]: We believe that politics is a part of the Religion, and those who try to separate the Religion from politics are only attempting to destroy the Religion and to spread chaos.

[14]: We believe there will be no honour or victory for the Muslims until they return to the Book of Allāh and to the *Sunnah* of the Messenger of Allāh (ﷺ).

[15]: We oppose those who divide the Religion into trivialities and important issues. And we know that this is a destructive *da'wah*.

[16]: We oppose those who put down the knowledge of the *Sunnah*, and say that this is not the time for it. Likewise, we oppose those who put down acting upon the *Sunnah* of the Messenger of Allāh (ﷺ).

[17]: Our *da'wah* and our *'aqīdah* is more beloved to us than our own selves, our wealth and our offspring. So we are not prepared to part with it for gold, nor silver. We say this so that no one may have hope in buying out our *da'wah*, nor should he think that it is possible for him to purchase it from us for *dīnār* or *dirham*.

---

[1] From *Fiqhul-Wāqi'* (p. 49) of al-Albānī.
[2] From *Fiqhul-Wāqi'* (p. 51) of al-Albānī.

[18]: We love the present day Scholars of the *Sunnah* and hope to benefit from them and regret the passing away of many of them. Imām Mālik said (d.179H) - رحمه الله, "The knowledge of *hadīth* is your flesh and blood and you will be asked concerning it on the Day of Judgement, so look who you are taking it from."[1]

[19]: We do not accept a *fatwā* except from the Book of Allāh and the *Sunnah* of the Messenger of Allāh (ﷺ).

These are glimpses into our *'aqīdah* and our *da'wah*. So if one has any objection to this, then we are prepared to accept advice if it is truthful, and to refute it if it is erroneous, and to avoid it if it is stubborn rejection. And Allāh knows best.

---

[1] Refer to *al-Muhaddithul-Fāsil* (p. 416) and *al-Kifāyah* (p. 21) of al-Khatīb.